THE HISTORY AND DEVELOPMENT OF SMALL ARMS

by

A. J. R. Cormack

Published by
PROFILE PUBLICATIONS LTD.
Windsor. Berkshire, England

Copyright © Profile Publications Ltd. 1982.

ISBN 85383 085 1

First published in 1982 by
PROFILE PUBLICATIONS LIMITED
65 Victoria Street, Windsor, Berkshire, England.

Printed in Spain by Heraclio Fournier, S. A.
Vitoria-Spain

CONTENTS

Acknowledgments

The author would like to thanks the following for their help, without which this volume would not have been possible. Herb Woodend of the Pattern Room at Enfield, the late Frank Hobart, Andrew Yule and Pierre Claude Tilley.

The Percussion Era led to the extensive hobby of target shooting. Shown here are two Percussion Target Pistols made by Le Page of Paris
Wallis & Wallis

A Guide to Small Arms

by A J R Cormack

The Oxford Dictionary definition of the term 'Small Arm' is simply 'a portable firearm'. This is a guide to the history and development of these weapons. In Part One the history of the Military Small Arm is traced from the hand cannon to the modern gas operated rifle and machine gun. From the simple muzzle loading pistol to the efficient automatics which equip the soldier of today. In Part Two the technical development and types of action and systems of operation are described. These developments are traced showing how each had their effect on the weapons.

The tank met its match with the adoption of such weapons as the Piat shown here. The weapon is being loaded with its spigot fired hollow charge bomb
Imperial War Museum

Part 1

**A Brief History of the
Development of the Small Arm**

A fully equipped Infantryman carrying
a SIG rifle
S.I.G.

The application of gunpowder in a small arm dates
from about 1320. The early hand held weapons
featured a long tiller rather than a stock. This tiller
was held under or over the arm when the weapon
was fired or even leant against the ground or wall.
The reason for the tiller, apart from its being a
handhold, may also have had something to do with
the unreliability of the weapons of the time which
called for brave men as it was far from unknown for
the gun to blow up on firing. The knights of the time
delegated the firing as being beneath their dignity,
but one can only wonder!

All these early handguns were cannon ignited with
the attendant disadvantages of the powder touch
pan. The stocks were made in one of three ways; an
iron rod as an extension of the barrel, a wooden
pole bound on to the barrel, and a pole that fitted
into a socket in the end of the barrel. Sometimes
there was also a protrusion on the barrel to help in
holding the weapon. Aiming of the gun at this time
was not really possible as the firer had to hold the
match and the weapon, then apply the match to the
touch hole, meanwhile having kept the priming both
in the pan and dry! All this in the heat of battle gave
him more to do than aim.

The date of the first pistol, or 'one hand gun' is more
difficult to pinpoint as the definition of the weapon
rules out the guns with tillers, and those which were
made in the shape of small vases, modelled on the
full size weapon, were hardly what one could call a
'one hand gun'. The use of a slow match really rules
out any form of pistol as two hands were definitely
needed and the gunners of the time would probably
have been thankful for three.

Multi-shot weapons of the cannon ignition type
can be either superimposed load working in a
similar manner to the Roman candle or of the
multi-barrel type. There are a number of multi-barrel

handguns which feature a group of barrels made up
in a bundle and attached to a tiller. Each barrel had
its own touch hole and thus had to be primed before
firing. The soldier could at least now fire more than
one shot without the cumbersome reloading. A later
modification of the system uses pan covers that
keep the powder dry and in place.

The multi-barrel weapon with cannon ignition
survived a long time and the organ type batteries
later used were the forerunner of the machine gun.
These weapons used as late as the American Civil
War often featured cannon ignition. Interesting
comment on the reliability of the early multi-barrel
weapons can be seen in the 'Holy Water Sprinkler'
type of weapon that has a mace head containing the
barrels so that if the gun did not fire one could
always brain the opponent. The guns of this time
were used mainly to frighten the enemy rather than
to inflict massive casualties.

The invention of the matchlock and the elementary
form of trigger made the handgun more of a weapon
to be reckoned with. The soldier did not have the
difficult job of trying simultaneously to see the
enemy and find the touch hole with the slow match.
The weapon could at last be aimed in the direction
of the enemy with some degree of certainty. The
pistol became a possibility but very few have
survived and many of those that are found are of a
much later time. This type of ignition was used by
the inhabitants of the remote parts of India and
China at a much later date when the rest of the
world had progressed. The handgun at this time
developed a stock that meant it could be fired from
the shoulder or leant against the armour although
the pistol was characterised by the butt being
almost in line with the barrel. This must have made
aiming a difficult problem. The matchlock dates from
1400 apart from the above-mentioned exceptions,

6

A Bristol Gatlin Gun
—note the Martini—
Henry rifles
*City of Birmingham Art
Gallery and Museum*

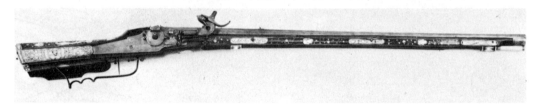

Even by 1620 the Wheellock Rifle was well-
developed. The above is a 32 bore Saxon
Wheellock and features six-groove rifling
Wallis & Wallis

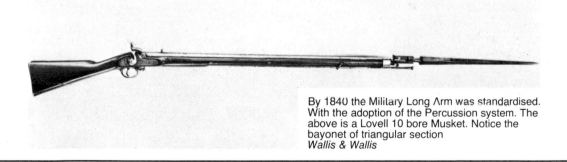

By 1840 the Military Long Arm was standardised.
With the adoption of the Percussion system. The
above is a Lovell 10 bore Musket. Notice the
bayonet of triangular section
Wallis & Wallis

One of the early Breech Loaders was the
Berdan
Smithsonian Institution

LIEUT.-COLONEL

Patrick Ferguson

Killed at King's Mountain

SOUTH CAROLINA

7th Oct. 1780

De H. Ed. Gestr. Heer
IAMES FERGUSON.
BRIGAD.-GENERAL, &c.
OBIIT XXII OCT.
MDCCV.

"IF AN ARDENT THIRST FOR MILITARY FAME,
A SOCIAL AND BENEVOLENT HEART,
AN UNCOMMON GENIUS,
A MIND GLOWING WITH PATRIOTIC FIRE,
REPLETE WITH USEFUL KNOWLEDGE,
AND CAPABLE
OF PERSEVERING UNDER DIFFICULTIES
WHERE GLORY WAS IN VIEW,
CLAIM OUR ADMIRATION;
THE FATE OF
MAJOR PATRICK FERGUSON,
WHO POSSESSED THESE AND OTHER VIRTUES
IN AN EMINENT DEGREE,
AND WHO FELL
WARRING AGAINST DISCORD,
IRRESISTIBLY
CLAIMS OUR TEARS."

"THE TORY TULIP-TREE."

BRIGADIER FERGUSON'S GORGET.

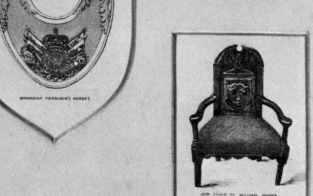

ARM CHAIR OF WILLIAM FORBES.

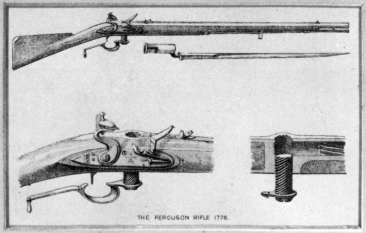

THE FERGUSON RIFLE 1776.

The standard armament of both Indian and Cowboy—
the Winchester '73. This weapon provided the combatant
with a means of repeated fire
National Film Archive

◄ Many attempts were made to improve the muzzle loading
Flintlock. The above shows details of the Ferguson Rifle
and also some history of the designer
United Services Museum

and was superseded in the early part of the 17th
century by the wheellock. The rifled barrel became
known but, because of the cost and complications of
manufacture with the primitive machines available, it
was not widespread. This development led to an
increase in accuracy which was not passed on to
the soldier of the time.

With the invention of the wheellock the soldier had
at last a reliable pistol and musket. The weapons
took on distinctive shapes, the musket now standard
with the butt that could be rested against the
shoulder and the pistol which still had the butt
almost in line with the barrel. There was often a ball
at the end of the butt or in some cases a 'swelling'.
These were not, as the shape suggests, an
instrument for braining the enemy, but either a
means of withdrawing from the holster or a
decoration. The breech loader was developed even
if it was a little dangerous as the problem of breech
sealing was not solved for some time. The reliability
of the weapons increased although the existence of
weapons with either a matchlock of a wheellock or
two matchlocks for the one barrel would seem to
prove the fragility of the lock work. This fragility
made the simple matchlock more attractive to the
average soldier. The multi-fire weapon became a
more feasible possibility as the firing of the charges
could now be regulated instead of the chain reaction
of some of the early weapons.

In the reign of King Henry VIII the revolver was
developed with a wheellock. The cylinder was hand
turned but the basic principles were well developed.

One of the early Lever Action weapons was the
Burnside. This particular weapon is in the
Smithsonian Institution Patent Collection
Smithsonian Institution

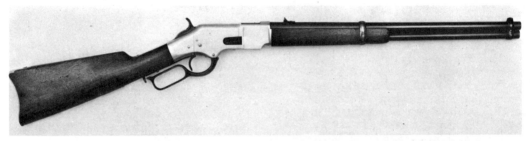

One of the most advanced of the Lever Action
Weapons and certainly the most famous was the
Winchester. This is a Model 1866 Carbine
Winchester Gun Museum

Other forms of multi-fire weapons were the chain fire with multi-barrels and the superimposed load with multiple locks. The multi-lock weapons often had three or more complete locks each connected to fire a load. The accuracy of the weapon also made a target weapon a possibility as the firer could now concentrate on the target and worry less about the firing mechanism. The decoration of weapons reached a high point and many of these beautifully finished pieces have survived. This is explained by the custom of the rich of the day giving highly decorated weapons as gifts and the prestige of owning such a weapon. These survived, as many such collections were handed down through the family, unlike the plain weapons of the soldier which, when obsolete for the purpose of war, were scrapped and thus did not survive.

The second half of the 16th century saw the development of the Snaphance lock and with it the shape of the weapons became almost fixed. The pistol now became the common modern shape with the butt at a more acute angle to the barrel and thus aiming became a possibility. The reliability of the weapons made them more and more important in battle and this type of lock was more 'soldier proof' than the rather fragile wheellock. The addition of the automatic pan cover, pan covers having been in use for some time, made the weapon reliable in wind and rain. This did, however, add to the complication and was mainly used on the more expensive guns. The Scottish pistols have survived in reasonable numbers as they have the unusual feature of the butt being made in metal. These weapons exhibit a class of decoration, common on the surviving weapons. All the forms of multi-fire weapons were used in a similar range of types to that of the wheellock.

On the Mediterranean coast the development of the Miquelet lock was important as the combination of the frizzen and the pan cover made the firing of the weapon as simple as, but less complex in action than the Snaphance with automatic pan cover. This simplification was however marred by the adoption of an external main spring although this did make repair easier. The shape of the weapons was now fully confirmed and the weapon outline varied little from this time on.

The adoption of the true flintlock with its internal lockwork and combined frizzen and pan cover led to development of most of the ideas that were to come in the percussion era. The weapons now featured a variety of methods of loading in both pistol and long arms, such as screw-off barrels, breech loading with hinged chambers and magazine repeaters such as the Lorenzoni. The barrels of the better types were rifled and the sporting weapon became a well-developed group. The soldier for the most part had to be content with a muzzle loaded smooth bore weapon. The duellist on the other hand had a beautifully balanced rifled barrel pistol which was superbly accurate. Target shooting became a well-established sport and the rifled barrels made the weapons accurate at improbably long ranges. The use of the rifled barrel for the soldier was pioneered by the Americans in the War of Independence when their long-barrelled

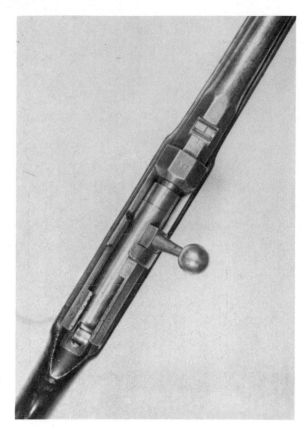

A Dreyse Needle Gun. The simple construction is evident

Pennsylvanian Long Guns proved the winners at extended ranges. The weapons, both pistol and longarm, remained for the most part as muzzle loaders. The multi-fire weapons reached an advanced state of development with the revolver, turnover barrelled, superimposed load and tap action weapons. The firearm was now the weapon of the masses and not just the rich.

Percussion Weapons

The invention of the percussion lock by the Reverend Forsyth was the signal for the speeding up of the development of the complete group of small arms. The Forsyth Scent Bottle Lock on both long guns and pistols is extremely rare but, because for the first time the firer could aim and fire without the delay of the earlier locks, this was the vital development which led to all other types of percussion weapons.

The Forsyth lock was developed for a sporting gun and the majority that remain are of this type.

The percussion lock developed in numerous ways, with pellet locks, pill locks, tube locks and cap locks, as well as numerous weird and unlikely alternatives. This was an age of experiment and the results were in some cases bizarre and impractical. The percussion system allowed the breech loader to flourish with all its variations. There were, even in this transitional period, numerous breech loaders and attempted multiple fire weapons, but few were produced in any quantity and thus the soldier did not benefit to any extent. The rifled barrel was now

Infantrymen crossing a road barricade. Equipped with SIG SG510-4 Rifles fitted with bayonets. Notice also the grenades carried by the jumping soldier
S.I.G.

well-established among the more expensive weapons and particularly in the better quality sporting guns, although the military weapon, for reasons of price was often still a smooth bore.

The true percussion weapon with the percussion cap made both the breech loader and the multi-fire weapon reliable and common. The percussion cap made the revolver a much simpler weapon and so reliable that the more advanced nations accepted it for their troops albeit in limited quantities. The open frame revolver developed initially gave way to the solid frame, the loading although still from the muzzle now had the advantages of numerous extremely practical rammer systems, and just as many impractical ones too! Automatic loaders that not only measured out the powder (flasks had been doing this for a long time) but also inserted the ball or bullet into the chamber were developed. The cylinders were, for this type of loading, removable and also could be capped by automatic cappers.

The pepperbox now became a formidable weapon as, with the revolver, the trigger mechanism became reliable in both single and double action. The difference between the pepperbox and the revolver is that the pepperbox's barrels revolve as a complete unit and on the revolver the cylinder only turns.

The pepperbox and the revolver came in a variety of shapes and sizes, some pepperboxes having many barrels. The hammer was designed on both to work from all conceivable angles—top, bottom, side and back. The rifled barrel and the adoption of sights,

even if both had not attained the modern sophistication, made the weapons very accurate and with the ability to fire six or more shots, the soldier had at last an efficient pistol.

The longarm now had rifling and although still for the average soldier a muzzle loader in the early days of percussion, the inventors started what was to be a field day of efficient and in many cases the very opposite in breech loaders. The first thought of the military was to convert the existing stocks of percussion muzzle loaders into breech loaders, and weapons such as the British Snider became the infantryman's friend. He could now fire faster and with reasonable accuracy. These weapons served the soldier well and such variations as the revolving rifle, not only with the standard cylinder but with vertical and horizontal flat cylinders, and even with a primitive belt feed in the form of the chain gun, met with some success. The single shot now started its development with innumerable different breech systems. The multi-shot longarm was in limbo as the use of the percussion cap did not lead to many improvements and thus development stagnated.

The volley gun remained the basic weapon although the powder train was sometimes ignited by a percussion cap. The Billinghurst Requa battery gun was such a weapon.

The invention of Nicholas Dreyse's bolt action needle gun made the military cartridge firing bolt action weapon a fait accompli as the rival armies who opposed the Prussians learned to their cost. Attempts were made to duplicate the system in a

11

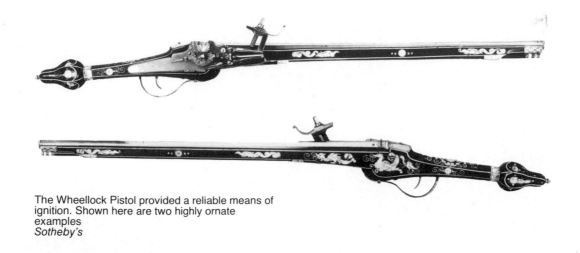

The Wheellock Pistol provided a reliable means of
ignition. Shown here are two highly ornate
examples
Sotheby's

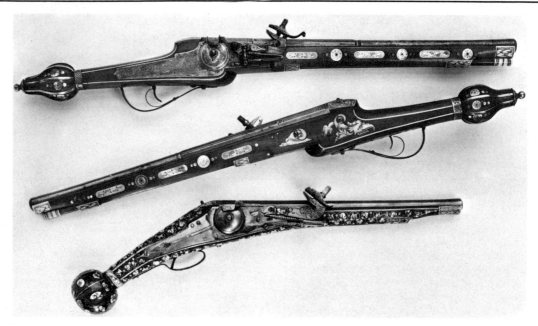

The Wheellock Pistol appeared in many forms.
Notice how the shape descends to become more
modern type. These pistols are of Saxon origin
Wallis & Wallis

pistol but they were not a success. The
disadvantages of gas leaks at the breech and burnt
needles because of the fact that they had to pass
through the powder to the primer led to the demise
of the system.

The bolt action rifle, however, was established as
the military weapon, a position it was not to lose
until the self-loader came into use.

The pinfire, with all the disadvantages of the
projecting pin, made the revolver a practical
cartridge loader, considerably easing the problem
when speed was important, although loading was
complicated by the need to position the pin in a slot
in the cylinder. This pin made the other multi-fire
developments almost impossible and no practical

systems except the revolver were evolved. The
longarm was also developed as a revolving type but
saw little use. The pistol on the other hand saw
some limited military use although the development
of the more practical rimfire soon superseded it. The
Belgian Arms Manufacturers did, during the pinfire
era, manufacture many thousands of cheap and in
some cases shoddy revolvers.

The invention of the self-contained cartridge was the
final catalyst that was needed to perfect the infantry
small arm. The rimfire was the invention which
achieved this and made it the most used cartridge in
the world today albeit for sporting use. The
first weapons that used the system were the
so-called saloon pistols, single shot weapons used,

The Scottish Clansman favoured the all-metal pistol. Shown here is a superb example of the so-called Doune Type. This pistol features an all-metal frame and butt and a button trigger
W. A. Craig

A Pocket Pistol of the Flintlock Era. Notice the large bore which at close range would inflict extremely serious injuries. The Decoration and butt cap are of a high quality
W. A. Craig

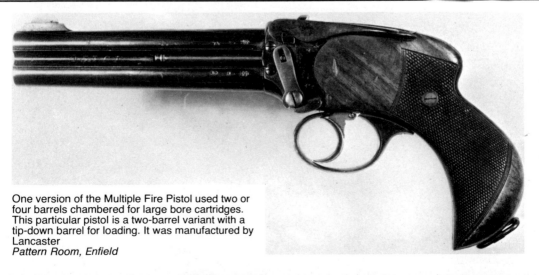

One version of the Multiple Fire Pistol used two or four barrels chambered for large bore cartridges. This particular pistol is a two-barrel variant with a tip-down barrel for loading. It was manufactured by Lancaster
Pattern Room, Enfield

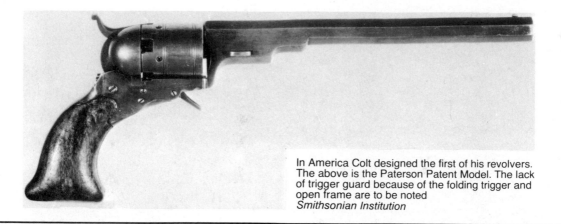

In America Colt designed the first of his revolvers. The above is the Paterson Patent Model. The lack of trigger guard because of the folding trigger and open frame are to be noted
Smithsonian Institution

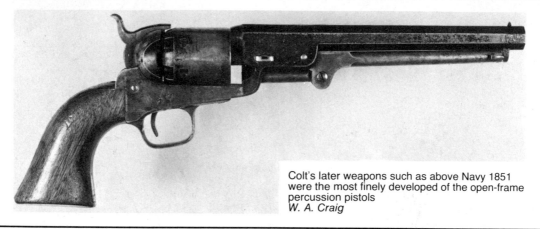

Colt's later weapons such as above Navy 1851 were the most finely developed of the open-frame percussion pistols
W. A. Craig

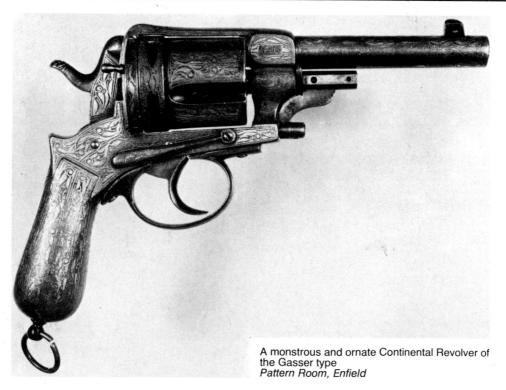

A monstrous and ornate Continental Revolver of the Gasser type
Pattern Room, Enfield

often indoors, for target practice. This pistol type remains in use in many much modified forms on the pistol ranges today. The military use of the rimfire in the pistol field was limited, as the Smith and Wesson ·22in swing up barrel was of little use because of its small calibre. Despite this, however, the basic development was complete. The military longarm took an important step forward when the Volcanic rifle was redesigned to handle a ·44in rimfire cartridge and the Winchester followed and saw practical use in many armies. The combination of a reliable rimfire and the later centre-fire cartridge and an efficient lever action allowed the soldier to fire as fast as he could aim. The military, always notorious for lagging behind in equipment, in many cases still stuck to the single shot admittedly breech loaded. This did have some reason, in that the rimfire repeater did not have the range of the single shot. The bolt action weapon now became a weapon which could receive popular acceptance by the soldier. (The Dreyse as noted had the problem of gas leakage). Such weapons as the Swiss Vettereli which combined the tube magazine of the Winchester and the bolt action was, with its modified rimfire cartridge, a military weapon to be reckoned with. The pump action became a reality and such weapons as the Winchester remain with little modification in production today.

The development of the centre-fire cartridge made the military revolver a first class weapon that was to remain in service with the major powers until the 1950s and indeed is in present service with many smaller powers. The loading methods as with the breech loading rifle were legion. The first side loaders which required the single ejection and loading of each round gave way to the break action with later, automatic ejection. This could be applied to break frame revolvers only, and so the swing-out cylinder typified by the modern Smith and Wesson and Colt weapons was developed. Such attachments as automatic extractors, worked by the action that ejected the empty round as it was fired,

were tried and rejected. The automatic revolver such as the Webley Fosbery was tried and, although showing some promise of success, was dropped for its simpler rivals.

The single shot rifle developments included falling, rising and rolling block and hinged breeches in innumerable types, the number of variations only being limited by the ingenuity of the designers. These had started with the rimfire in some cases but now the centre-fire cartridge made the single shot a long range and reliable weapon. The single shot did not last as a military weapon as the need was for a weapon that would fire faster. However, such names as Sharps, Peabody and Martini-Henry became famous.

The bolt action was now perfected and the systems of Mauser, Rubins, Mannlicher, Level, Lee and Ross all saw their adherents. The bolt action took the world through two major wars and numerous small conflicts as the main weapon of the average soldier. Magazines for the bolt action progressed from the tube to the almost universal box magazine and, on the later types, detachable boxes and clip loading. The bolt action rifle is still in service today in some small countries but its prime use is either as a sniper weapon with the major powers or a target and sporting weapon throughout the world.

The multi-fire weapon had only been waiting for this development and the machanically operated machine gun became possible. The hand-cranked Gatling gun and its many contemporaries all made formidable weapons but the tragedy was that the military did not appreciate their worth and thus the weapons suffered from misuse and in some notable cases lack of use. Colonel Custer would surely have lived longer if he had appreciated the worth of such a weapon against the massed attack of the Indians. The mechanical machine gun reached its final stage of development with the Gatling and its rivals being perfected, and indeed was to disappear with the advance of the recoil and gas operated developments. The Gatling however returned in the

A typical example of the British Percussion Open Frame Pistol. Notice the inherently weak structure with the lack of a top strap
Pattern Room, Enfield

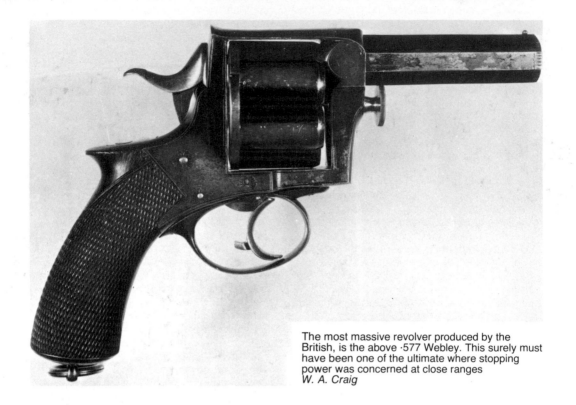

The most massive revolver produced by the British, is the above ·577 Webley. This surely must have been one of the ultimate where stopping power was concerned at close ranges
W. A. Craig

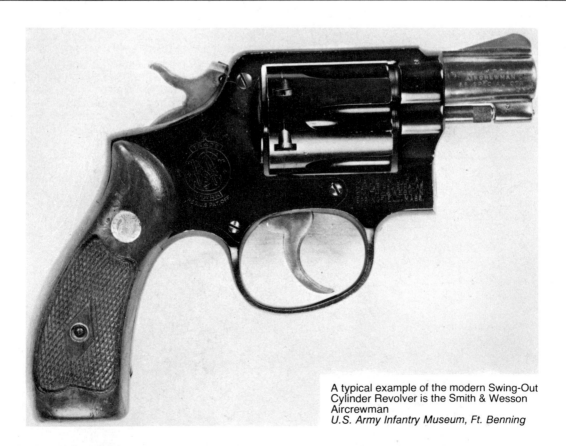

A typical example of the modern Swing-Out Cylinder Revolver is the Smith & Wesson Aircrewman
U.S. Army Infantry Museum, Ft. Benning

Hugo Borchardt was one of the first of the
automatic pistol designers. The weapon
shown has the optional shoulder stock
Wallis & Wallis

Typical small automatic pistol as used by
the Italian Forces in World War II—The
Beretta Model 1934
Author's Collection

60s as the electrically driven rapid fire gun; this development was not new as Gatling himself had used this source of power. The centre-fire cartridge with the increased strength and thus more power had given military weapons both long range, reliability and rapidity of fire.

The development of the self loading rifle began in the 19th century although ideas had been expressed a long time before. The first serious attempts utilised the well known and tried principles such as the lever action. The great Hiram Maxim started experimenting with the Winchester lever action, utilising the force of the recoil to work the action. The butt of the weapon was made to move inwards when the recoil drove it against the firer's shoulder; this in turn, by means of a lever connecting the stock to the action, drove the lever forward to work the action. A recoil spring then drove the stock back to its normal position and pulled the lever back, chambering a fresh round. This made a simple recoil-operated self loader which, considering the date 1831–33, would have been a considerable advance on any weapon then in use if it had been adopted. Ferdinand Mannlicher followed the 1884 patent of Maxim which had covered a recoil-operated locked breech machine gun, with a patent for a selective fire locked breech short recoil-operated rifle. Maxim continued his developments and in 1891 developed a weapon with a short stroke piston operation. Mannlicher meanwhile developed a number of different weapons between 1891 and 1900. None of these weapons was developed although many of the basic design features were to appear later. This led the late W. H. B. Smith, the renowned firearms expert, to state that Mannlicher's work was underestimated. In this same period John Browning entered the field of automatic rifles with a muzzle trap design. This system which has had little success, uses a cone to trap the gases at the muzzle and, by attaching the cone to the breech block, the gases are used to work the action.

Mauser, although he had the best bolt action rifle in the world at this time, saw the direction of the development and designed a rifle with a long recoil operation. This, along with developments by Browning at about the same time, met with no success from the military point of view. Difficulties of the system and the fact that the action had to extend so far back defeated it. These long recoil weapons were under development from 1898.

In Britain the Griffith and Woodgate rifle was tried in 1894. This was a locked breech weapon with a turning bolt which had the requisites of a military

A hand-cranked machine gun provided the earliest form of controllable repetitive fire. This example is the Gatling Gun
City of Birmingham Art Gallery & Museum

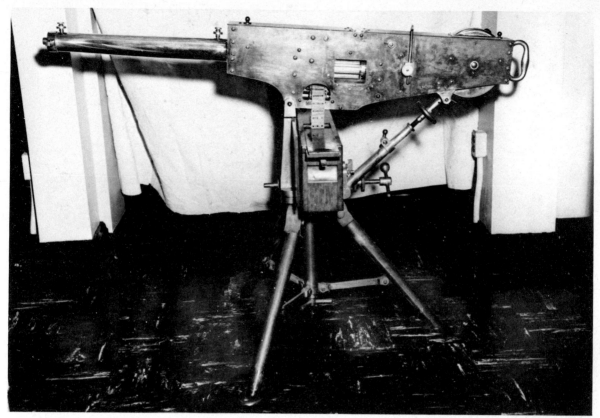

Maxim was one of the first of the true Machine Gun designers. The above is his Patent Model
US Marine Corps Museum, Quantico

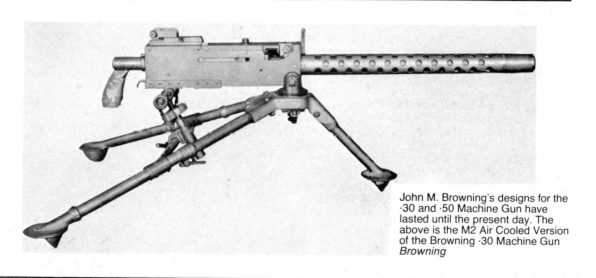

John M. Browning's designs for the ·30 and ·50 Machine Gun have lasted until the present day. The above is the M2 Air Cooled Version of the Browning ·30 Machine Gun
Browning

weapon but failed to achieve success through lack of development following no official interest.

The Italians developed a self-loading rifle in 1900, the Cei-Rigotti. This was an advanced weapon featuring a gas cylinder and piston that operated the breech which had a rotating bolt with front locking lugs. The Danish Bang used the Mannlicher and Maxim developed muzzle trap design and was sufficiently promising to be tested by the American Government. The French carried out a number of experiments from 1898 until the outbreak of war in 1914.

It will be seen from the above that the First World War could have been fought with self loading rifles if the military had allowed them to be developed. The lack of interest in the development of self loading rifles was to last through the inter-war years and except for limited use in the Second World War when the majority of soldiers were still equipped with the bolt action weapon, it was not until the post

19

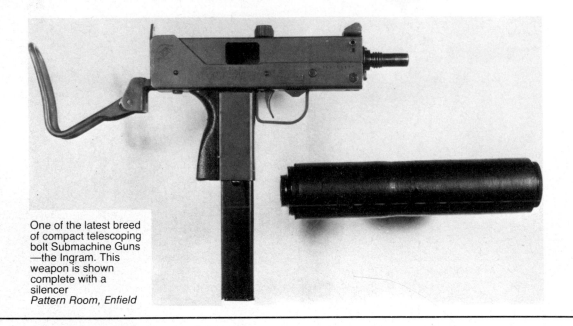

One of the latest breed of compact telescoping bolt Submachine Guns —the Ingram. This weapon is shown complete with a silencer
Pattern Room, Enfield

war years and the 50s in particular that they were universally adopted.

The First World War saw the adoption of some self loading weapons in limited quantities, and although the inter-war years were not very productive, the Second World War saw the finalisation of the design although not the adoption. The post war years saw the adoption of the self loading rifle as the standard weapon of the major powers. The developments are best understood if they are enumerated country by country. The Germans adopted two self loading rifles for use from their aircraft during the First World War. The Swiss firm of SIG had developed the Mexican designed Mondragon rifle, a gas-operated weapon, and although it was not a complete success proving to be sensitive to dirt, it was used in limited numbers. The second weapon was the Mauser 7·92mm Aircraft Self Loading Carbine which was a recoil operated weapon. The between war years saw little development although Mauser did produce one 7·92mm rifle, the Model 35. The Germans therefore entered the Second World War with no standard self-loading weapon. There had been some development in cartridge design and this resulted in the idea of an assault rifle or short cartridge being adopted in principle by some sections of the German forces. The development of a rifle for the cartridge was delayed by the machine gun doctrine of the army and the orders of Hitler. Thus although the actual ingredients of the weapon were there it was not until 1942 that the MP43/44 series of gas operated tilting bolt weapons were put into production. Although the start was late, development was swift—the FG42 gas operated rotating bolt design followed. This weapon in particular was an assault rifle of advanced design and only the lack of production towards the end of the war stopped the adoption of this and the MP44 in larger numbers. There were other designs, the

Mauser developed Gewehr Model 43 a crude but effective gas operated rifle, the Mauser experimental StG45M which was to be the forerunner of many of the post war designs, the VG1-5 experimental gas retarded blowback rifle, and many other weapons made in experimental quantities only.

When able to re-arm the German Government expressed interest in the Spanish CETME which was a development of the Mauser prototypes of the

The General Purpose Machine Gun can if necessary be fired in an advancing roll
Crown Copyright

1   A British soldier armed with an early model Thomson Submachine Gun. Notice it is fitted with a drum magazine
2   German combat troops fording a stream. Notice the MP18 Submachine Gun carried by the rear soldier
3   A German Machine Gun Crew in operation during the Second World War. It must have been extremely uncomfortable for the forward soldier as the barrel is only two inches from his ear. Notice also the soldier at the rear is carrying an MP40 Submachine Gun.
Imperial War Museum

22

war years. This weapon, developed by Heckler & Koch was adopted as a standard weapon for their army. The Spanish CETME was the rifle which bridged the development of the wartime Mauser developments and the present day roller lock weapons.

The Swiss, after the production of the Mondragon by SIG, continued with development after many attempts at self-loading rifles, including the novel blowforward AK53 SIG, adopted the SIG development StGW57. This weapon uses pivoted rollers to lock the action and is the best finished full-power cartridge-firing weapon of the current standard weapons.

With the introduction of the short rifle small bore cartridge, the ·223in, a development of the locking system was used in the SIG530. This utilises the gas system to control the rollers.

The Italians developed two self loading rifles before the Second World War. Neither were produced in quantity. The 6·5mm Scotti-Brescia Model X (1931) which saw very limited use in the war and the Breda Model 1935, a selective-fire rifle manufactured in limited quantities for the Army. After the war, Beretta developed a number of rifles, all based on the American Garand, and later initially developed a ·223in weapon in conjunction with SIG. This Beretta rifle has a simple rotating bolt with gas action.

The French, after the St Etienne-developed rifles; the Model 1917 and 1918 which were both turning bolt gas operated weapons (later because of unreliability converted to simple straight pull bolt action), developed no weapons of any interest. The present gas operated weapons have no distinguishing features but the newly developed weapon for the ·223in cartridge may prove more noteworthy.

American development did not really start in earnest until the end of the First World War when such weapons as the Thompson, a development of the Blish lock, the first of the Garand developments, primer actutation in a similar way to the Danish Bang, the Pederson, of great interest as the Pederson cartridge ·276in was an attempt to produce a small bore design, and lastly the weapon that was to be the standard issue in the American Army, the gas operated Garand, made their appearance. The Johnston turn bolt recoil operated rifle which was entered into a trial with the Garand in 1936 was not a success as it really required further development, but it was the first use of the short recoil system in a military rifle to have any success

as some were used during World War II by the American Marines.

The post war developments were varied but the next weapon to receive approval was the M15, a development of the Garand. This was followed by the direct gas operated Armalite-designed and developed AR15. This weapon is of great importance as it introduced the ·223in Armalite cartridge. The direct gas operation encountered difficulties but these were overcome and the cartridge became the one that other countries used as their standard for development of small calibre rifles. This cartridge is a considerable advance on any that the Allies had used in the wars, as the only small calibre one in quantity use was the M1 carbine ·30in. (This was only increased power pistol round and thus made the M1 carbine a short range weapon.) The Stoner concern, with Eugene Stoner acting as the designer after his stay at Armalite where he had designed the AR15, came out with a weapon system based on a gas piston as opposed to the direct gas system of his previous design. This weapon has not as yet been accepted and the Armalite concern have a similar type of weapon on offer known as the AR18. Both these weapons have been developed as part of a family of different application weapons and although they as yet have not been adopted in any quantity they represent typical present development.

The Russians started development of the assault type rifle as opposed to the full-sized automatic rifle as early as 1916 with the Federov-designed short recoil weapon. The Russians developed numerous rifles with gas operation and either wedge or rotating bolt systems. They surprised the Germans in the Second World War with their use of the designs of Tokarev and Simonov and drove the Germans into development of weapons to counter them. The gas operated SKS followed, which utilised a tappet operated tilting bolt. The present Russian Weapon, and for that matter the weapon that is used either directly or in derivatives by most of the Communist world is the AK47. The AK uses a 7·62×32mm cartridge which with the gas operated rotating bolt, straight line stock, low recoil, makes this the model assault rifle.

Great Britain after the second World War decided to adopt a new cartridge and a rifle to suit. The final cartridge decided upon was the ·280in and the weapon the EM2. The EM2 was a gas operated weapon of the bull pup design firing the short ·280in round. The unusual shape of the weapon with the magazine behind the pistol grip with the resultant straight line stock made it particularly controllable on automatic fire and generally very easy to handle. The Government, after deciding to adopt the weapon, which had successfully competed with weapons in the early stages from BSA and later from America and Belgium, were persuaded by American influence to adopt the 7·62mm cartridge which was to equip NATO. The EM2 could not be converted with any speed or success as it was designed to fire the assault rifle type of cartridge and the Government decided to adopt the Belgian FN rifle. In retrospect with the adoption of the ·223in round this must be considered as a mistake.

---

1   The Belgian designed GPMG in action with the British Army. Notice the spare belt carried by the Gunner
Crown Copyright
2   The enemy is no longer safe even in the dark. This soldier is firing a General Purpose Machine Gun equipped with Night Sight
Crown Copyright
3   British soldiers shown in winter conditions firing a GPMG from the prone position
Crown Copyright
4   The tank more than meets its match when the Infantryman is armed with a Carl Gustaf 84mm Recoilless Rifle
Crown Copyright
5   An Armalite AR18   Rifle firing a rifle grenade. This type of firing has largely been superseded by the Grenade Launcher
Armalite Inc.

The Belgians after developing a number of rifles with Browning designs adopted the M1949 gas operated weapon. This was superseded by the FAL which was to equip not only the Belgian Army but also among many others, the British. This is a tilting bolt gas operated weapon chambered for the 7·62mm NATO cartridge. The weapon is the one most used outside the Communist Bloc. FN have also developed a rifle for the ·223in cartridge

There are a number of other designs indigenous to various countries such as the Swiss SIG530 and 540 but none has achieved the great production number of the FN FAL and the AK and its developments which, along with the AR15, equip the majority of the world's armed forces.

The first attempts to produce a self-loading pistol were adaptations of the revolver principle using either recoil or mechanical means to work the action. The Bitner was such a weapon using a trigger to operate the action. The idea of recoil action had been explained in print some time before the actual use. The Austrians in 1892 developed the Schonberger, a delayed blowback design utilising primer set back and used what was for that time an advanced metallic cartridge which was clip loaded through the top of the pistol. At about the same time another inventor, Andrea Schwarzlose, developed a short recoil rotating bolt pistol firing a 7.63mm cartridge dimensionally similar to the Mauser round but not as powerful. The forerunner of the famous Luger was invented by Hugo Borchardt; this was a toggle action and although a successful weapon it did not receive any military support. The pistols of Theodore Bergman were developed at about the same time, i.e. 1893–97. The Bergman pistols saw some use and featured a falling block recoil operated design. In 1896 the first of the Mauser designed pistols which saw limited military use in both wars was introduced.

This pistol had many of the features to make it far from an ideal military weapon such as clumsy shape and expensive and complicated manufacture. It was well received however and received publicity as one, if not the first, of its kind to be used in battle, when no less a person than Sir Winston Churchill used it in the Boer War. A fully automatic version was manufactured which could take the place of the submachine gun. The early Mannlicher models were chambered for a straight-sided case which was amply powerful for the delayed blowback action. The pistols manufactured by the Steyr concern of Austria are well made but received little military interest. The later Model 1903 was chambered for a bottle-necked cartridge with similar dimensions to the Mauser 7·63mm. As the weapon was still of the delayed blowback type and the delay was very little, the construction of the pistol of a light nature the Mauser cartridge would damage the weapon.

The Webley range of pistols which were developed from the Mars were either of the locked breech type for the powerful ·455in Webley automatic pistol cartridge, or blowback for the others. The massive but dependable Webley in calibre ·455in auto saw service with the British in the First World War, but because of its complexity and size it was dropped for the simple and, in view of many of the military,

more reliable revolver. The one man, who, more than any, made the military automatic pistol an accepted weapon was John Browning. The pistols developed by Colt and FN have become the side arms of many armies and the derivations of many more. The Browning recoil operated locked breech design as implemented on the Colt ·45 model 1905, modified on the 1911 and finalised on the 1911 A1 was to become one of the standard systems of automatic pistol design. The link controlled locking rib type of operation is used on such weapons as the Spanish Star and the Russian Tokarev, as well as other copies of the Colt. The Tokarev design deserves a mention as the complete hammer group of components can be removed in a field strip for cleaning and the cartridge feed is machined into the receiver. These are both important modifications of the basic design.

The last of the Browning designs was the Browning Hi-Power. This weapon, while using the locking lugs of the earlier design, replaced the links with a cam. This simplification and the extra large magazine capacity have led to its adoption by Britain and many others as their standard military weapon. The French M1935 and the Swiss SIG both use a modification of the Browning design similar to the Hi-Power. A derivation of the basic design is the Polish Radom that has a recoil spring guide that protrudes through the slide on recoil.

The Walther designed P38 has a simple falling block that is cammed out of engagement to allow the breech block to recoil. It also features for the first time on a mass produced military weapon a double action trigger. This pistol with its 9mm Parabellum cartridge became the standard side arm of the German army during the Second World War and is still in service today as well as being sold commercially.

The Japanese Nambu features a similar type of lock and has a minimum of parts not rivalled by many pistols of the locked breech type. It is however very badly manufactured.

The straight blowback weapons are too numerous to mention and by and large did not become standard military issue, although some use was made of the Spanish Astra. The delayed blowback weapons such as the Italian Glisenti were chambered mostly for low-powered cartridges and thus ineffective for military use although used for such. There are a number of military pistols which have used other than the standard methods of operation and have been accepted and put into service in some number. The Austrian Steyr 1912 features a rotating barrel lock and fires an extremely effective cartridge the 9mm Steyr which is similar to the ·38 ACP. This weapon also saw use in the Second World War when the Germans rebarrelled it for the 9mm Parabellum. The use of the clip-loading system is a drawback but such innovations as a means of emptying the magazine by a button are an improvement. A derivation of this lock system is used today by the French firm of MAB.

The Hungarian Frommer uses the long recoil system which is overly complicated. The actual use of such a system in a ·32 ACP automatic with its revolving breech block is a testament to man's

A standard German side-arm for the latter part of
World War II was the Walther P.38
J. Bowman

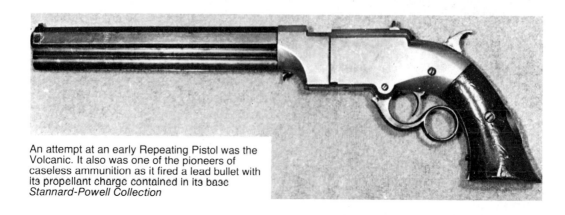

An attempt at an early Repeating Pistol was the
Volcanic. It also was one of the pioneers of
caseless ammunition as it fired a lead bullet with
its propellant charge contained in its base
Stannard-Powell Collection

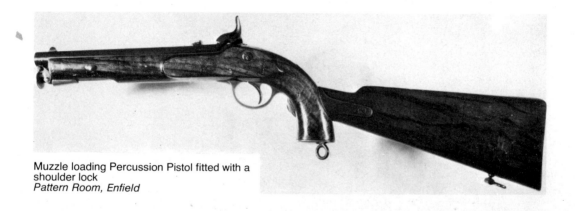

Muzzle loading Percussion Pistol fitted with a
shoulder lock
Pattern Room, Enfield

attempts to make the job at hand more difficult than it is considering the fact that the pistol could have been a simple blowback.

The self-loading pistols in use today by the various armed forces are by and large developments of or original designs by the great John Browning. The Belgian Browning Hi-Power is used by many forces including Britain, the Colt ·45 1911A1 by the American forces, the Star by Spain, the SIG by Switzerland, the Tokarev and its derivatives by the Communist world are all based on the patents of Browning. There are exceptions such as the P38 Walther and the H&K P9, the former with its falling block and the latter a roller delayed blowback system. The remainder such as the Soviet Mokarev are blowback types.

The submachine gun was developed to give the soldier an easily portable compact light rapid fire weapon. The initial attempts were made by providing pistols such as the Luger and Mauser with a shoulder stock and in the case of the Luger an extra large magazine.

The weapon to be given the credit as being the first true submachine gun is the Villar Perosa Model 1915. This is a twin barrelled weapon delayed blowback operated, firing the 9mm Parabellum round. The weight of the weapon makes the title incorrect as it is heavy and not easily portable. The Germans however realised the importance of the submachine gun and developed the Schmeisser MP18. This was the true submachine gun as it featured the essentials, blowback operation for simplicity and cheapness, plus light weight and compact dimensions for ease of use.

The Vollmer, developed by the firm of Erma, and its successor the EMP were built on similar lines to the Bergman but used the telescoping main spring, a feature that was to be used in the later MP38 and MP40 weapons.

The rest of the major powers did little development and regarded the submachine gun as the weapon of the gangster. This attitude was fostered by the development by Auto Ordnance of the Thompson submachine gun. The prototype weapons were produced before 1919 when the first production weapon utilising the Blish lock was introduced. After trials in 1920 by the Army, Auto Ordnance continued to develop a number of weapons but it was not until the Second World War that the Thompson was adopted by the military. The Russians waited until 1926 to start development of the submachine guns but rapidly adopted them with such weapons as the PDD, PPSh41, PPS42/43. During the Second World War the Russians used submachine guns in vast numbers. In Germany the Schmeisser MP18 was developed by Bergman into a range of weapons and the Vollmer was finally streamlined into the superb MP38 and finally MP40 submachine guns.

In Italy the Villar Perosa gave way to the Beretta Model 18. This was to be the first of a long line of simple, efficient and compact weapons developed by Beretta.

Great Britain although entering the field very late did so with a weapon that was easily the most efficient from the point of view of manufacture and cost. This was the Sten Gun. The initial weapons did however leave much to be desired from the point of view of safety. However, the essential ingredients were developed into the Post War Sterling Submachine Gun. The Americans also adopted an ultra simple weapon in the M2, often called the Grease Gun. The Swiss developed a number of submachine guns mainly from the SIG concern, all of which featured folding magazines. It must be noted that as the submachine gun is the simplest of all weapons to construct being little more than a barrel, a recoil spring and a bolt, there are innumerable variations

1 The Platoon Mortar of the Second World War, the 2″. This weapon is shown being fired at a low level trajectory.
Imperial War Museum
2 Even during the Second World War the Infantryman was not powerless against the tank. Although the anti-tank rifle was not particularly effective. Shown is an ambush position in a damaged house, the soldier on the right is shown firing the Boys Anti-Tank Rifle, on the left the soldier has a Grenade Launcher fitted to his rifle
Imperial War Museum
3 The 81mm Heavy Mortar being fired under practice conditions
Crown Copyright

The Infantryman with his own weapon. A modern self-loading rifle
Crown Copyright

By the Second World War the Infantry Weapon had reached an advanced state. The above is a typical late production

FG.42 German Assault Rifle or Light Machine Gun. Notice the extensive use of pressings and stampings
Lowland Brigade Depot

One of the lastest generation of weapons. The Fabrique Nationale LAR ·223 Rifle
FN

made either in official Government workshops or by local underground organisations.

The submachine gun of the 1970's is little different in its basic concept to the Schmeisser MP18. The only major improvements are that most of the weapons are safer to handle and the modern stamping and welding techniques are utilised to the full. Such weapons are the Israeli Uzi which is manufactured by Fabrique Nationale of Belgium (as well as in its native country), the Italian Beretta M12 and the American Ingram. The one development of note is the telescopic bolt.

A new breed of weapon is making itself known. This is the delayed blowback or locked breech either recoil or gas operated ultra short rifle which fires the assault rifle type cartridge. Two such weapons are the Heckler & Koch HK53 and the Colt XM177E2. The main advantage of this type of weapon is that two types of ammunition are not required as the submachine gun and the assault rifle both fire the same cartridge.

The father of the machine gun was Hiram Maxim who started in 1883 with a short recoil system of operation which initially locked the bolt to the barrel. By 1885 the weapon had become a short recoil utilising a toggle joint and featuring a belt feed. Although the British in 1887 used a Vickers manufactured Maxim in trials, little or no interest was expressed. Vickers however continued to modify the basic design. The Germans not only developed the weapon but adopted it in great numbers. This to a large extent explains the casualties in the First World War when complete battalions of troops were wiped out trying to cross barbed wire infested No Man's Land under cross fire from machine guns.

Vickers although given little encouragement continued development and finally the machine gun which was to last as the sustained fire weapon of the British Army through World War II and into the 50's was accepted for use in the British Army. John Browning realised early on that the days of the hand-cranked machine gun were over and in 1889 designed his first gun featuring a muzzle trap method of operation. This was quickly succeeded in 1895 by the well-known 'Potato Digger' Browning which was operated by gas piston. The reason for the name is that the piston extension during operation projected downwards; thus if the gun was mounted too near the ground it tended to dig a hole. The weapon which was to be used by the American Army during World War II was a modification of the next development, the model 1917 which was a short recoil locked breech weapon with water cooling. A further model, the Model 1919, was developed which was identical to the Model 1917 but featured air cooling and a changeable barrel. The final modification was the uprating of the weapon to fire the ·50in machine gun round. This was first water cooled and then air cooled with the designation M2.

Colonel Isaac Lewis designed in America the well-known Lewis gun which, finding no interest, he offered in 1914 to BSA. This gas operated air cooled drum fed machine gun was standard British issue until the Bren Gun in 1939.

Both the Japanese and the Italian machine gun development can be summed up largely as featuring odd-feed systems, often blowback operation with oiled cases, coupled with bad manufacture and unreliable operation.

The Russians produced three noteworthy machine guns. The Degtyarev Type DP, a gas operated weapon with a projecting lug lock; the Goryunov medium machine gun which was gas operated and featured a Bren-gun type lock and finally the RPK which uses a gas system and a rotating bolt lock. These Russian weapons are by and large reliable under combat conditions although in many cases crudely manufactured.

Two interesting weapons featuring unusual methods of operation are the 1912 Schwarzlose and the Madsen. The Schwarzlose is a delayed blowback weapon with the delay brought about by the mechanical disadvantage in a link system. The Madsen which was produced from 1900 until the

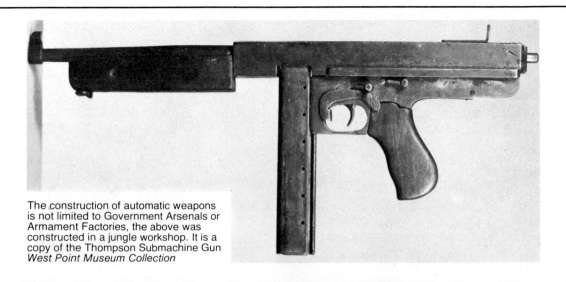

The construction of automatic weapons is not limited to Government Arsenals or Armament Factories, the above was constructed in a jungle workshop. It is a copy of the Thompson Submachine Gun
West Point Museum Collection

1950's features a system that at first glance would seem to be impossible, however, as the weapon has received extremely wide distribution over a long period of time it must function relatively efficiently. The action is a modified Martini type with the breech block moving above and below the line of the cylinder bore. On the down stroke the weapon is loaded and on the up stroke the empty case is ejected. The operation is of the long recoil type controlled by a cam plate.

The German Second World War development has influenced many of the present day designs. The MG34 is a recoil operated weapon with a rotating bolt. A double method of feed was used, either a double drum or a belt. The MG42 was a roller locked recoil operated weapon with two very desirable features, namely construction by metal stamping and a very advanced belt feed system which, by keeping the loading on the belt and drive pawls low, leads to very reliable operation. This weapon now named the MG3 is standard with the German Army today.

The FG42 is a highly portable weapon, fired from an open bolt on full auto fire for cooling and closed bolt on single shot for accuracy.

The first gas operated machine gun was the Hotchkiss. This weapon, the original design of which was dated from 1895, was used in both World Wars by the French. A gas operated piston connected to the breech block forces the locking pins out of their recesses. The weapon is clip fed.

The French developed one of the oddest light machine guns, the Chaucat. This weapon was a long recoil weapon with a rotating bolt and was fed from a curved magazine fitted under the weapon. The best known and probably most reliable and efficient light machine gun is the Bren. The name comes from the development of the Czech BRno ZB26 made by the Royal Small Arms Factory at ENfield. This is a gas operated, box fed tilting bolt weapon of the very best type.

The latest developments feature many of the basic designs of the Second World War and the light machine gun now fires in some cases the ·223in round. The 7·62mm NATO and its equivalents however remain the favourites for most LMG's and GPMG's and the ·50in Browning and its equivalents for the HMG's. The FN L7A2 GPMG is standard with the British Forces and features a gas operated tilting bolt action. The venerable Bren gun now chambered for the 7·62mm NATO round is still in limited use. The American Forces use the Browning designs but have conducted many experiments with such weapons as the Stoner. The American M60 GPMG utilises features from both the MG42 and FG42 weapons. The Swiss SIG concern and the German H&K both offer roller or lever delayed blowback weapons.

In all weapons, the rifle, LMG, GPMG, HMG and SMG, there is a tremendous amount of experimental work continuing at this time, the main avenue being the development of a cartridge to supersede both the 7·62mm NATO and the ·223in Armalite when they reach obsolescence. The spearhead of these developments is directed at the lightweight rifle cartridge, as the 7·62mm NATO and its equivalents are officially thought of in the role of light machine gun cartridges. The Communist Bloc already have their short round although they too are experimenting with small calibre rounds. Most current lines of research are on the small and ultra-small round i.e. 3·5–6·5mm. The basic actions of these new weapons, however, exhibit little change.

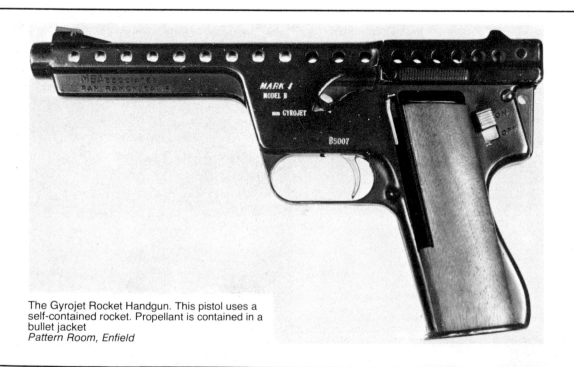

The Gyrojet Rocket Handgun. This pistol uses a self-contained rocket. Propellant is contained in a bullet jacket
Pattern Room, Enfield

An experimental Mauser rifle firing caseless ammunition
Mauser

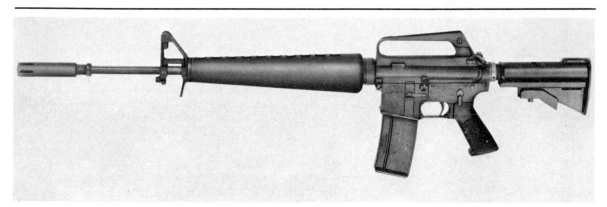

A telescopic stock version of the M16. It is fitted with a nylon magazine
Sherwood

The British EM2 rifle that set a trend for some of todays weapons

CAPTIONS FOR PAGE 32

Top Left:
Comparison of the Mauser
caseless ammunition
with a conventional round
of the same calibre
Mauser

Top Right:
The Israeli Galil which
fires the 5.56 M193 round
from an action similar to
the AK47
I.M.I.

Middle Left:
A Nylon magazine for the
M16 rifle
Sherwood

Bottom Left:
The experimental Steyr
Daimler Puch rifle
S.D.P.

A range of small calibre weapons with their attendant cartridges has emerged in the anticipation of a new range of small arms for the 1980s.
As yet most are of a conventional type that is to say they use a standard cartridge construction and a conventional projectile. The M.16 of which four million have been produced has a large following especially with the 'optimised' 5·56mm cartridge. The French have announced a delayed blowback rifle, the MAS which is chambered for the standard 5·56mm M193 round but can obviously be rechambered for any similar round. The rifle is unusual in that it is a bullpup design i.e. the magazine is behind the trigger guard and there is no stock as such. This configuration leads to a very short overall length with a full length barrel. The one disadvantage is that the firer has the breech next to his face, probably more psychological disadvantage than a practical one. The weapon makes extensive use of plastics and steel pressings. The delayed blowback relies on a lever system as with the French GPMG.

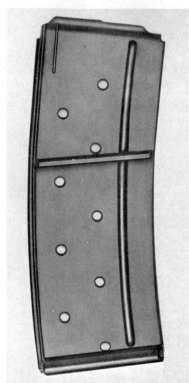

The British entry for the 1980s is also of a bullpup type but fires a new 4·85mm cartridge which has superior ballistics to the 5·56mm. The operation of the weapon is conventional gas type similar to the AR18 Armalite with a multilug rotating bolt. The construction is conventional with metal pressings, plastic hand guards but also uses investment castings.
The German firm of H&K have two weapons, a conventional rifle firing a new 4·6mm×36mm round and a small calibre non-conventional rifle firing a caseless round. The first is of conventional pressed construction and uses the well tried roller delayed blowback action. The trigger gives controlled burst fire capability and the ammunition is loaded in a thirty round prepared box. The caseless ammunition and weapon system are still on the restricted list but it is claimed that the problems associated with caseless ammunition such as cookoff chamber erosion have been solved.
It is probable that a new range of light machine guns will follow these new rifles and the British already have such a weapon. One company the Sterling Armament Co. of England have announced a group of weapons including a rifle, a bullpup rifle, an interchangeable barrel light machine gun all chambered for the 5·56mm cartridge and based on the AR18.

Part 2

Chapter 1

Gunpowder and On

The invention of the basic components of a firearm was spread over a long period in history and as with many inventions it was dependent on the application of a series of known facts rather than a sudden discovery of the whole.

The actual constructional materials for the early weapons such as wood, Iron, phosphor, bronze, etc, were known much earlier than the invention of the gun as were techniques of construction. The one ingredient, however, which was not discovered until the early thirteenth century was a propellant or, as it is known in its simplest form, Gunpowder. The actual date of its invention or even, for that matter, the inventor of gunpowder, are shrouded in mystery. Misinterpreted writings and, above all, theories expounded by experts based on incorrect and unsubstantiated facts have become legends over the years. The experts did not purposely wish to mislead but the writings on which a lot of the evidence is based have lost their true meaning through 'embroidery' or 'misinterpretation' in successive translations.

In 1260 a Friar, Roger Bacon, in one of his works chronicled what is believed to be the first recorded formula for gunpowder. Bacon's formula contained an anagram which has had various translations but which most experts agree used charcoal, sulphur and, most important, saltpetre. Why Bacon chose to use an anagram can only be guessed at. Perhaps he felt that the world was not ready for the possible dangers the knowledge could bring.

Where Bacon's knowledge came from is doubtful, but he did not invent gunpowder, he merely chronicled its invention. The inventors of gunpowder are often supposed to be the Chinese but the writings on which this is based are now doubted and Arabic writings are given more credence. Bacon could have obtained his ideas from either Chinese or Arabic sources and even now among the experts there has been little agreement as to the exact time and place of its invention. Further claims have been made for India as that country has natural saltpetre deposits. One real problem to the translation of the original documents has been that 'Greek Fire' (pitch and saltpetre) which was used as an incendiary and fired from bows, catapults and ballistas sounds only too like a gun when described as 'belching forth fire and smoke'. As Green fire was known about 700 AD this has led to inaccuracy in translation which dates gunpowder wrongly or attributes it to the wrong inventor.

It can be said that the knowledge of gunpowder probably came to Bacon from Arabic or Chinese sources, either of which, with India, have claim to the invention.

The most popular name for the inventor of gunpowder, derived by legend and not by fact is either Marcus Graecus or Berthold Schwartz. Marcus The Greek as with all legends is a misty and indistinct figure who apparently knew the formula for black powder considerably earlier than all other claimants. Black Berthold or Berthold Schwartz, as with Marcus Graecus, is a figure shrouded in mystery and the most accurate picture of his experiments would seem to be similar to Shakespeare's famous Witches' Brew in 'Macbeth'. It would not be acceptable for the inventor of such a thing as gunpowder to have a common name and therefore, by popular desire and by perpetuation of the myth, the name Marcus The Greek or Berthold Schwartz will continue.

Gunpowder made the gun possible by providing a propellant. Gunpowder's earliest use was probably as a firework and as such the constituents were mixed in fairly random amounts. Only later when applied as a propellant and an explosive was the composition standardised. The difference between a propellant and an explosive is at first sight not vast as it is merely the rate of burning. However, if a propellant burns too fast in a gun an explosion results with the obvious and unwelcome consequences.

Gunpowder's rate of burning depends on two facts, namely its composition which varied continually until the eighteenth century, and the size of grain. Because of saltpetre's hydroscopic qualities, attempts were made to make the very fine powder less liable to become damp. This led, in the early 1600s to gunpowder being manufactured in larger grain sizes called corned powder. Corned powder was made by wet mixing and grinding the constituents then leaving them to dry, when the result could be divided into constant grain sizes. Later still, prism powder was manufactured and this continues up to the present day. One of the advantages of corned and/or prism powders is that they can be separated into sized lots and thus specific burning rates.

One disadvantage of black powder is that the chemical reaction of the burning is incomplete and leaves a deposit in the barrel. This deposit, apart from being corrosive owing to its salt content, makes each shot successively tighter in the bore and with a muzzle loading weapon this led to the third or fourth shot being impossible to ram down and in turn to the use of undersized bullets and a resultant lack of accuracy which continued until the adoption of smokeless powder.

Although gunpowder is no longer used as a commercial propellant it has a large following of enthusiasts who continue to use it for sport.

The difference between smokeless and gun powders is first indicated by the name, secondly by the aforementioned lack of deposit, and finally by its increased efficiency.

The two discoveries which made this possible were those of guncotton and nitroglycerine. These form the basis for the smokeless powder. The former, also called nitrocellulose, was discovered about 1845 by C. F. Schoenbein in Germany who mixed cotton with nitric and sulphuric acids, the resultant cellulose nitrate being washed and forming guncotton, or with more nitrogen providing the basis for smokeless powders. The latter, made well known by Nobel, was invented by Sobrero in Italy at about the same time as guncotton. Nitroglycerine is an oily clear liquid manufactured by mixing concentrated nitric and sulphuric acids and glycerine to form glyceraltrinitrate which is the chemical name for nitroglycerine. This was used to make dynamite. Although nitroglycerine and dynamite are in them-

selves useless as propellants, being explosives, nitroglycerine can be blended with nitrocellulose to form a type of smokeless powder as well as Cordite, a much used propellant in large bore cartridges. These nitrocellulose based powders were first developed around 1867 and come in a variety of shapes and sizes in grains, sheets, balls and ribbon. Ball powder was invented by the Western Cartridge Company (part of the Winchester combine) which in 1930 experimented by dissolving nitrocellulose then washing it and finally hardening it into balls.

The outbreak of World War II speeded the development and finally in 1940 the process became a production possibility. Nitrocellulose either manufactured or obtained from old powder was dissolved in ethyl acetate with a protective colloid which stops the liquid recombining into grains thus leaving the powder in various sized balls. These are combined with extra nitroglycerine, dried and finally coated with a deterrent to control the burning speed. This powder is now in general use especially in American military ammunition. Experiments to develop a substitute for powder have been made utilising gas or liquids. Even advanced forms of electric power such as lasers have been used in an attempt to supersede the bullet and powder. However, until an economic, easily produced substitute arrives, powder will continue to be used.

Chapter 2   To Fire the Powder

Cannon Ignition

The Latin word Canna means a tube and thus the early weapons which were simply tubes often of bamboo bound with wire were called canna. The Infantry weapon was a hand canna or hand cannon. The earliest form of ignition was by lighting an incendiary at the muzzle of the weapon and letting it burn back round the ball until it ignited the charge of black powder.

A modification which was soon devised was a touch-hole at the back of the tube which enabled the powder to be fired by applying a lighted match or hot wire to the powder. ('Match' in this context means a slow burning prepared cord). Later a pan to carry priming powder was added which held the powder round the touch-hole. The cannon tube at a later date was often made with two diameters; one—the smallest and rearmost—held the powder and the other the projectile.

The early attempts were not a great success as the powder was not of any great power and the cannon ignition system of an open touch-hole on the barrel was at the mercy of rain, wind and even gravity if turned the wrong way up. If the gunner succeeded in keeping the powder dry and in the touch-hole, the projectile in the barrel and his match lit, the results were more of a firework nature than dangerous. Black powder fouling would have been a great problem as well as trying to keep the match lit. Often before a battle commenced, a fire was lit beside the gunner so that he had a guaranteed

method of ignition. If it rained, firearms were out, and in any case the long and crossbows were considered at least in the early days as being potentially more dangerous.

With all the disadvantages, the above system was still in use with hand cannon until 1400 and, with bigger weapons, until much later.

Matchlock

The matchlock was a logical development of the cannon lock as in its first version it was merely a means to hold the match on the weapon. The name of the person who decided to use a lever to lower the match into the powder is not recorded, but this led directly to the use of a trigger. It is interesting to note that the development of the trigger for the matchlock was surprisingly slow especially as the crossbow had long since had a well-developed one. As with the earlier cannon locks, the touch-hole was eventually moved to the side of the weapon where it was slightly more efficient. One improvement was the provision of a pan cover so that the user could at least keep the powder dry and in the pan. The cover, however, had to be moved by hand whenever a shot was contemplated. The early attempts at a trigger were simply an 'S' shaped lever pivoted in the middle. However, the later versions of the matchlock used a trigger mechanism with a spring so that the match was snapped downwards into the pan.

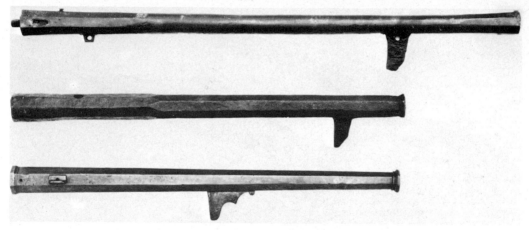

Three Hackbutts showing various forms of cannon ignition
Crown Copyright Tower of London

A simple matchlock shown
detached from the original
weapon. Notice the pan cover
*Crown Copyright, Tower of
London*

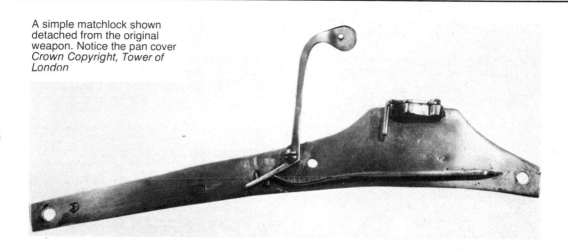

Wheellock

Why the wheellock should have been invented, or
Indeed by whom, will never be known. One theory is
that it originated with a tinder lighter. However, the
clockwork mechanism is easily explained as the
watchmakers of the day were very far advanced in
things mechanical. The wheellock system uses a
hammer which holds a piece of pyrites in contact
with an abrasive wheel. This wheel, when the trigger
is pulled, revolves, driven by a spring mechanism,
causing a shower of sparks. The shower of
sparks is guided into the powder pan and the
weapon thus fires. One of the first advantages of the
system was that while with the matchlock one's
position at night was clearly visible, and stories are
told of commanders using this fact either as a
means of locating enemy troops or by having
unarmed troops holding matches as a ruse, with the
wheellock this no longer applied. The use of pyrites
with a striker was to continue until the adoption of
percussion ignition, admittedly with the substitution
of a flint, marking an important step forward.
The knowledge of the striking of a flint to cause a

spark had been known since the Stone Age but its
application to the ignition of powder in firearms,
however arranged, was the turning point as far as
their use as practical weapons in military operations
was concerned. It will be noticed in the illustrations
that many of the wheellocks are very beautifully
decorated, and in fact most surviving weapons of
this age are of a similar nature. The explanation is
one not immediately obvious, except for the fact that
firearms of this period were a status symbol to the
rich who were the only people able to afford them
for hunting. A nobleman would not be socially
acceptable unless his armoury contained a number
of highly decorated pieces. As the noblemen
invariably handed down their possessions from
father to son, many of these richly decorated
weapons have survived.
A point to note on the reliability of the wheellock is
that many wheellocks were manufactured with a
matchlock as a second means of ignition. A large
number of wheellocks were also manufactured with
two hammers so that if the pyrites, which was easily
damaged, became ineffective in one hammer, the

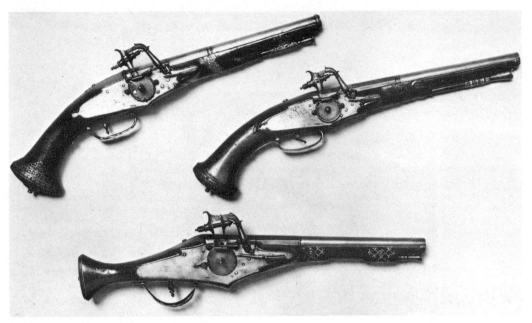

Three wheellock pistols. Notice the keyed spindle for winding up the wheellock
Birmingham City Art Gallery and Museum

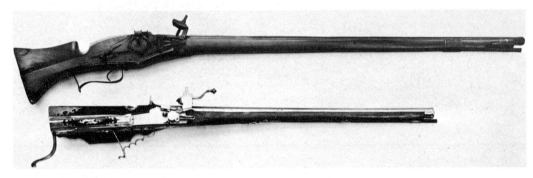

Top: A mid-seventeenth century 10-bore military wheellock
Bottom: A 28-bore Austrian wheellock dated 1730
Wallis & Wallis

other could be used. The ultimate disadvantages of poor metal and incorrect tempering for the spring which made it unreliable if kept wound, and the possible loss of the winding key, made the above precautions seem vitally necessary.

Snaphance

At first sight the Snaphance and its later descendants would seem to be simpler than the above and this illustrates invention by simplification of a basic idea. The simple flintlock system consists of a hammer carrying the flint downwards under spring pressure to strike a steel thus creating sparks to ignite the powder. This system dispensed with the clockwork mechanism and thus allayed the nagging doubt as to whether one had forgotten to wind up

before trying to shoot one's adversary! The flow of sparks was chanelled by the steel into the pan and the steel itself was spring-loaded into firing position so that the flint did not continually have to be adjusted or broken by the impact.

The first modification to the basic system was the adoption of a pan cover. This cover was at first moved by hand thus acting as a safety device. On later weapons the pan cover was automatically moved by the action of a hammer or trigger. The fact that the pan cover is a separate unit to the steel is the main identification feature of the Snaphance. The word Snaphance is derived from the Dutch words for a particular type of hen which makes continued pecking movements with its head similar to the action of the hammer. The Snaphance made the soldier equipped with one into a force to be reckoned with as, in either the long or short barrelled versions its fire, although inaccurate, was now reliable. The Snaphance still had the disadvantage of a complicated mechanism to uncover the pan. The development of the firearm was proceeding on a different but parallel line on the Mediterranean coast where the Miquelet or Mediterranean lock was developed.

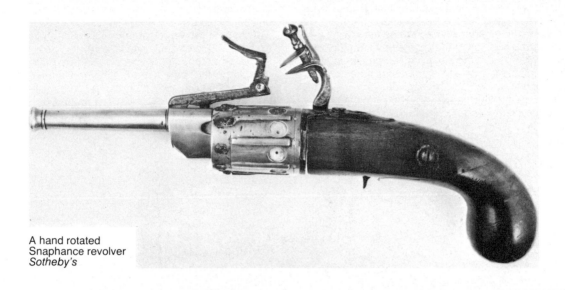

A hand rotated
Snaphance revolver
Sotheby's

A pair of Snaphance pistols. Notice the extremely ornate butt caps, trigger guards and lock plates
Birmingham City Art Gallery and Museum

The Miquelet

The distinguishing feature of the Miquelet lock is the massive external spring for the hammer. This would at first seem to be a retrogade step but when the slowness of communications at the time is realised, it can be understood that the internal lock spring was not well known to the gunmakers. The external spring may have been a disadvantage but the Mediterranean gunsmith had turned his inventive mind to the solution of the problem of keeping the priming powder in the pan. The two problems of keeping it in the pan and at the same time dry had been solved on the Snaphance with its complicated linked pan cover. The simplest answer to the problem was to combine the frizzen and the pan cover into one. This meant that the pan stayed closed until the frizzen was struck by the descending flint, thus ensuring that the powder was at all times protected. Needless to say, the most important step forward was the deletion of the complicated links and separate pan cover and the resultant increase in reliability. The combination of the frizzen and pan cover has also been attributed to the Spanish and as with many improvements it is difficult to pin point.

Throughout the development of the Snaphance and the Miquelet there had been many improvements to the trigger mechanism but the most important one, the adoption of a vertical sear instead of a horizontal one, did not come into use until the True Flintlock. It was left to the French to combine the best of the Mediterranean and Snaphance locks into the version known as the French or True Flintlock.

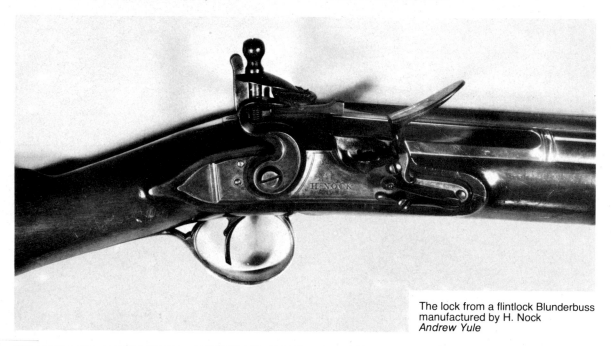

The lock from a flintlock Blunderbuss manufactured by H. Nock
Andrew Yule

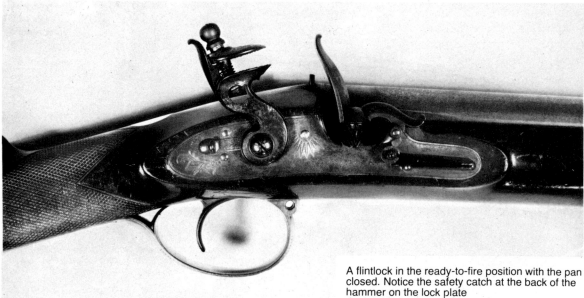

A flintlock in the ready-to-fire position with the pan closed. Notice the safety catch at the back of the hammer on the lock plate
Andrew Yule

The True Flintlock

The French combined the internal spring and mechanism with the combined frizzen and pan cover. The dating of the True or French Flintlock, unlike the other developments in the firearms field, is reasonably precise. The accepted date is between 1610 and 1615 and the probable place Normandy. The combination of the best of the Snaphance and the Miquelet by the use of the internal spring and mechanism of the one and the combined frizzen and pan cover of the other was the last modification of the lock other than to tidy up the design. The other French innovation was the substitution of a vertical sear instead of the horizontal one used in the other locks of the time. This led to the possibility of the positive half cock position with its advantage of safety as the weapon could be carried primed and ready to fire without the danger of a premature discharge.

The flintlock or its antecedents were the means of ignition until the great percussion patent of the Reverend Forsyth in 1805. The invention of the percussion lock did not oust the flintlock completely for some considerable number of years and has staged a comeback as a recreational sport in modern times.

Percussion

The author, being a Scot, must claim for his native land the invention of the first practical and true percussion weapon. The work of the Rev. Alexander John Forsyth has been little publicised and some authorities have cast doubt on his work being original. Even in his own day it took a publicity campaign by the *Aberdeen Herald* in 1839 to give Forsyth recognition. Parliament in 1840 debated whether he should be paid any reward and it was not until 1842, less than a year before his death, that the inventor-minister received his just dues.

The fulminates which made percussion a possibility had been known in the 17th century and the great Samuel Pepys mentioned them in his diaries of November 1663. The main problem was that the explosion created by the detonation of the fulminate led its users to try to use it as a propellant. As has been explained, if the propellant burns too fast it ceases to be a propellant and becomes an

---

The tombstone of the Rev. Forsyth in the churchyard at Belhelvie, Aberdeenshire
Author

explosive with disastrous consequences. It was left to Forsyth to develop a practical use for the fulminate and apply it successfully as a priming medium for the powder.

The Reverend Forsyth was born on 28 December 1768 in the Manse of Belhelvie, a village not far from Aberdeen. His father, the Rev. James Forsyth was Presbyterian Minister to the parish until his death in 1790, when his son Alexander Forsyth MD LLD took over the parish. Forsyth's hobby was shooting for game and he found that the delay between the pulling of the trigger and the ignition of the powder made game bird shooting very difficult as the bird had to be followed for a long time if the shot was not to be missed. The delay applied to any of the systems used and Forsyth set about improving them by using the fulminate to fire the powder.

The problems inherent in the use of fulminates to detonate the powder were twofold: one, that the fulminate must be protected from shock to prevent accidental detonation, and two, that a measured amount was used for each shot.

Forsyth used a powder magazine and at first a sliding device for measuring the correct amount of fulminate. This was a success but hardly a commercial proposition. His next attempt was a device which has become known as the 'scent bottle lock.' It is interesting to note that the patent he took out with the help of James Watt (Patent No 3032) in 1807 was to become a master patent as it covered not only the scent bottle lock, but sliding locks, a form of pin fire and finally a centre fired lock. This patent prevented, until its expiry, all further attempts in Britain to develop the percussion lock.

Forsyth was introduced through a mutual friend to Lord Moira, the Master General of the Ordnance, who, being most impressed with the scent bottle lock, decided that Forsyth should develop it for military use, as in its original form it would not stand up to the hard usage envisaged. A locum was arranged for the parish and the Reverend Forsyth moved to the Tower of London where a workshop was put at his disposal. Unfortunately when Lord Moira was superseded by John Pitt, brother of William Pitt, the Reverend Forsyth's services were deemed unnecessary. The scent bottle lock was tried at Woolwich in 1807 and although it functioned satisfactorily it was far from soldier-proof. After his return to his parish Forsyth decided to set up in business on his own account and employed a young gunsmith by the name of James Purdie who was later to go on to establish the famous gunsmiths business. The company manufactured sporting weapons until the death of the Reverend Forsyth in 1843. As with most geniuses his contributions to his craft were not realised until just before his death when the *Aberdeen Herald*, through extensive publicity, awakened an interest in his work and managed to persuade the Government to give financial assistance to his family.

The various inventions relating to the development of percussion firearms are by no means well documented. They also fall, because of the countries of origin, into no specific chronological or

The essence of the percussion system. The percussion cap, black powder and the projectile
Author

A pair of percussion pistols
W. A. Craig

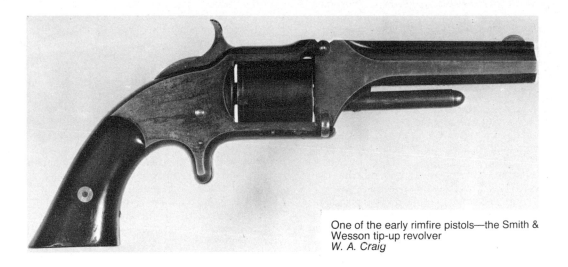

One of the early rimfire pistols—the Smith & Wesson tip-up revolver
W. A. Craig

A typical rimfire single shot target pistol
W. A. Craig

mechanical order.

At the time of Forsyth's death in 1843 both the centre fire, rim fire and pin fire had all been patented in various guises. After the scent bottle lock Forsyth manufactured a sliding magazine lock which utilised the same priming powder. The first of the other developments patented was probably by the Frenchman Prelat who, in 1810, patented in France a number of devices which were mostly copies or minor variations of Forsyth's principles.

In 1812 Pauly patented (Patent No 3833) the first centre fire cartridge. This used a long firing pin, almost a needle, which was used to detonate a primer compound contained in a paper cap at the rear of the bullet. There was no cartridge as such. Pauly is the inventor of the centre fire cartridge. One interesting patent taken out by Pauly was for the use of compressed air directed through a small nozzle to heat it up and thus detonate the fulminate. This technique is used by Daisy with their caseless ·22 ammunition, thus an old idea is used on an ultra modern weapon.

Joshua Shaw is normally given the credit for the invention of the percussion cap and his early development of a cardboard disc, quarter inch in diameter, with the priming compound in the centre was probably started around 1815. Because Shaw was an alien in the United States he was not allowed by law to patent his idea immediately and it was not until 1822 that he obtained his basic percussion cap patent.

Before the percussion cap a similar system was evolved using a pellet of priming composition either bonded together or wax coated which was detonated by the hammer. This system was patented by the British gunsmith Manton in 1816, Patent No 3895. Manton's design carried the pellet in the hammer as opposed to other similar systems in which the pellet was carried on the lock itself. This system had numerous disadvantages, the melting of the wax being a major one. Manton therefore developed a tube lock which operated by detonating a tube five-eighths inch long and one-sixteenth inch diameter containing the priming compound. This system, patented in 1818 (No 4285) was very reliable although it did by its very nature rule out any possibility of a repeating mechanism with a magazine feeding the primers. A development of the pill or pellet lock was the patchlock which was as the name suggests, a small patch containing the priming compound which was fitted to a special nipple. This system was the direct forerunner of Joshua Shaw's percussion cap. An interesting, if slightly dangerous sounding invention by a Frenchman, was to have the priming compound contained in a long tube, a piece of which was automatically cut off and advanced with each shot. This, in 1821, was one of the earliest attempts to use a magazine for priming other than the Forsyth types which were covered by his patents. Forsyth, almost fanatical in his pursuit of anyone who infringed his patent, which led to a number of law suits, did not do anything to forward the development of a magazine system as every turn was blocked by the comprehensive patents.

The straw continuous primer was followed by a copper tube version in 1834.

In 1821 W. Westly Richards with a Patent (No 4611) also came into the market with a pill lock, followed by a further patent in 1831 for an improved nipple for the pill lock. Westly Richards finally dispensed with the pill lock in 1842 when he patented a disc primer comprising a cardboard disc with the priming compound in the centre covered with foil. This was very similar to the development of Joshua Shaw who had finally obtained his patent for the disc in 1822.

The attempts at a magazine fed primer system were numerous, with attempts by Joseph Egg in 1822 and 1836 using a gravity fed pill lock and Joseph Manton in 1825 with a revolving primer feed.

In 1829 Pauly patented a cartridge which had its case made of metal and paper with a cap and nipple in the rear. This has been claimed as the first centre fire cartridge but the Pauly patent of 1812 would seem to be the correct claimant.

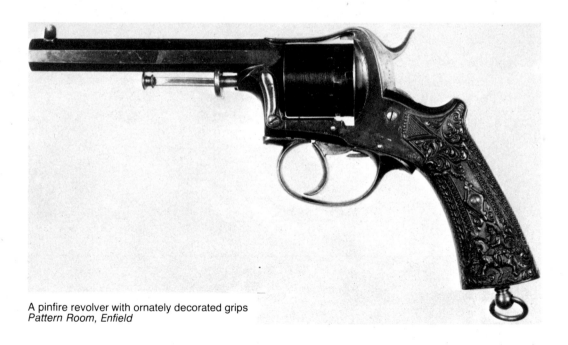

A pinfire revolver with ornately decorated grips
Pattern Room, Enfield

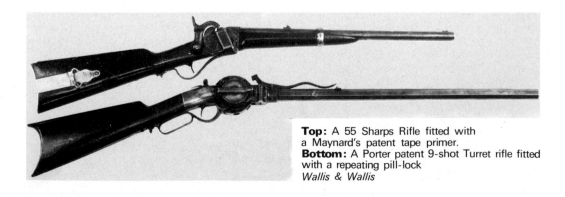

Top: A 55 Sharps Rifle fitted with a Maynard's patent tape primer.
Bottom: A Porter patent 9-shot Turret rifle fitted with a repeating pill-lock
Wallis & Wallis

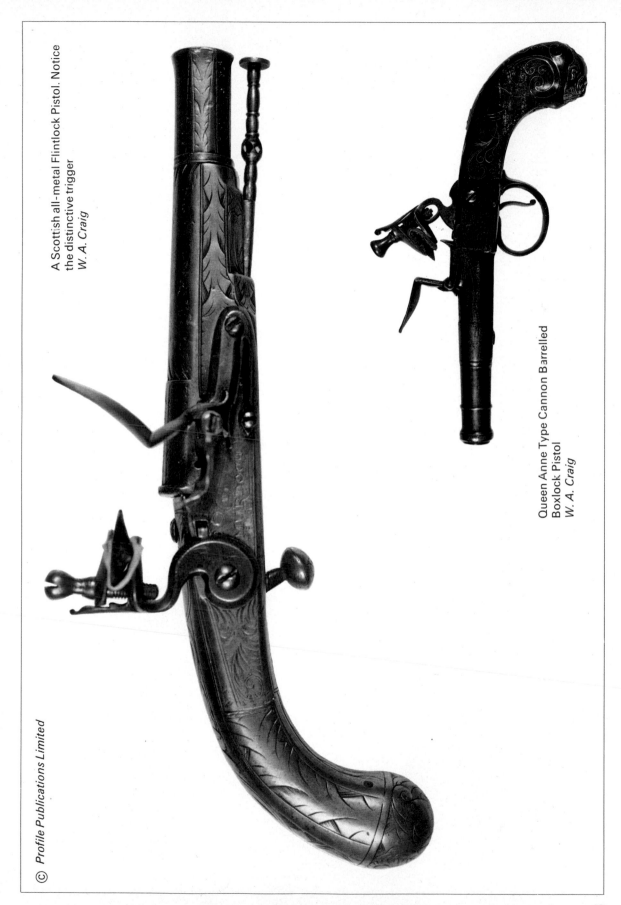

A Scottish all-metal Flintlock Pistol. Notice the distinctive trigger
W. A. Craig

Queen Anne Type Cannon Barrelled Boxlock Pistol
W. A. Craig

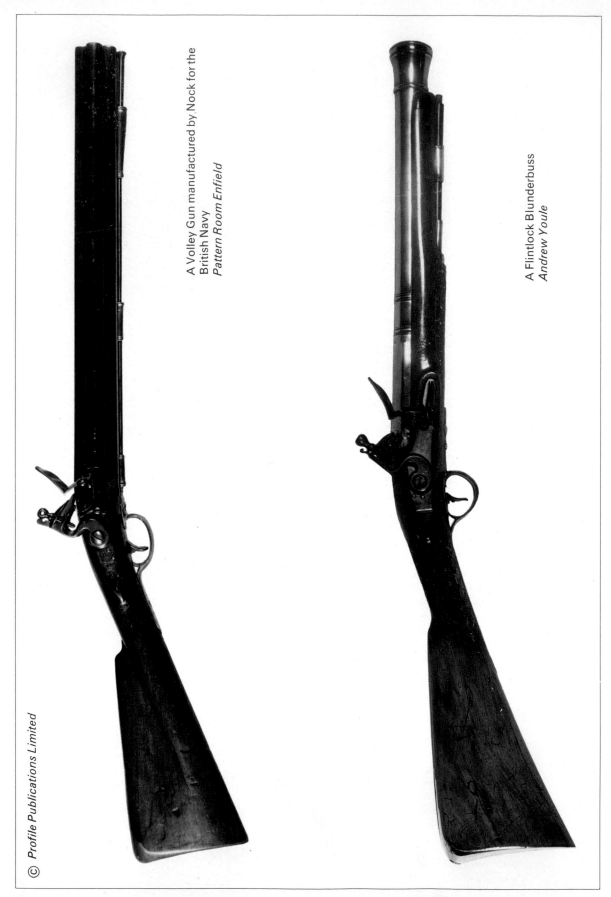

A Volley Gun manufactured by Nock for the British Navy
Pattern Room Enfield

A Flintlock Blunderbuss
Andrew Youle

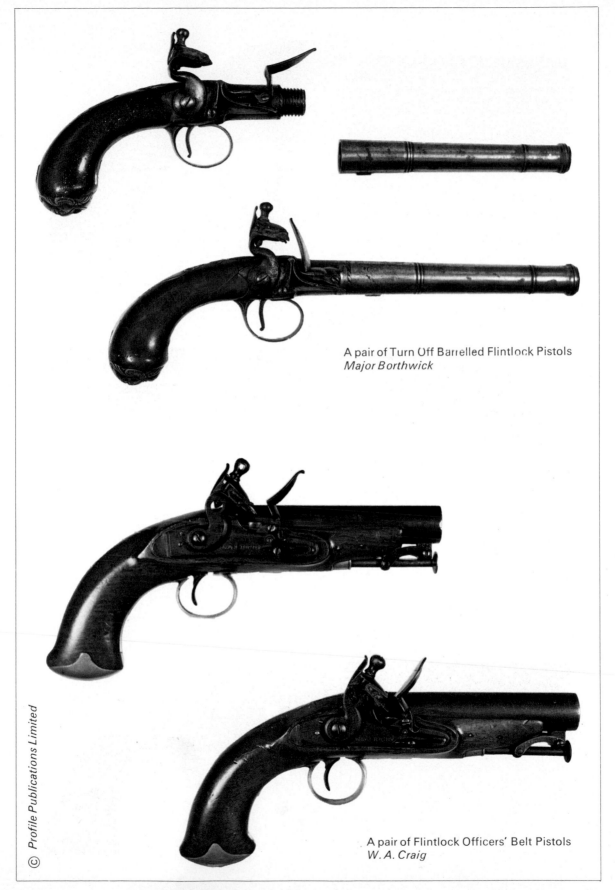

A pair of Turn Off Barrelled Flintlock Pistols
Major Borthwick

A pair of Flintlock Officers' Belt Pistols
W. A. Craig

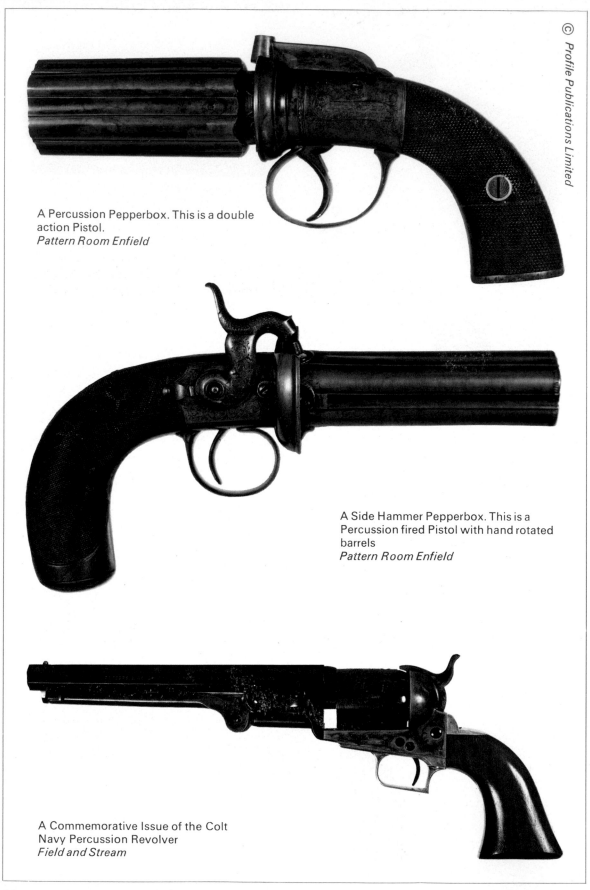

A Percussion Pepperbox. This is a double action Pistol.
Pattern Room Enfield

A Side Hammer Pepperbox. This is a Percussion fired Pistol with hand rotated barrels
Pattern Room Enfield

A Commemorative Issue of the Colt Navy Percussion Revolver
Field and Stream

In 1827 Dreyse patented his needle fire cartridge which owed a lot to the Pauly patents. This cartridge became famous because of the success the Prussians had when using it. The ability of an infantryman to fire his rifle as quickly as he could place a cartridge in the breech was a major factor in the Prussian success as her opponents had to depend for their part on muzzle loaders. The Dreyse cartridge, successful as it was, was not pleasant to use as the breech-cartridge combination was far from gas tight, thus allowing unpleasant blasts of hot gas to pour forth. This cannot have aided accuracy as the poor soldier was probably wondering whether or not he was about to be burned. Dreyse patented his needle fire in Britain in 1831 using Moses as his agent (Patent 6196).

To try to counter the problems of burnt out needles, escaping gas and actions choked with debris, the Frenchman, Le Francheau, devised a cartridge which had an internal primer which could be detonated by a pin passing through a small hole in the side of the case. This by its own description was

A percussion revolver of modern manufacture showing the nipples. Notice the sighting notch in the top of the hammer
George Wilson

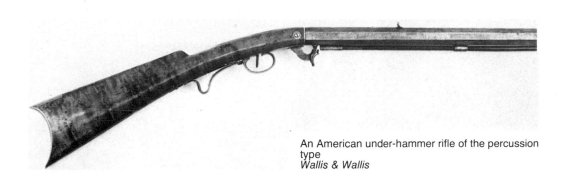

An American under-hammer rifle of the percussion type
Wallis & Wallis

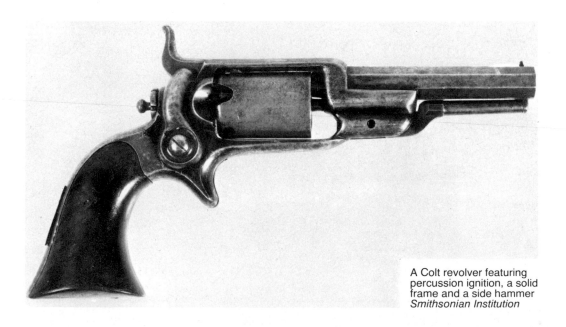

A Colt revolver featuring percussion ignition, a solid frame and a side hammer
Smithsonian Institution

A variety of modern experimental rounds. Multi-projectile, Multi-Flechette, Folded 5.56 mm.

One of the most modern double action revolvers— the Smith & Wesson 'Highway Patrolman'. Notice the swing out cylinder for ease of loading, the immensely strong solid frame and adjustable sights
Author's Collection

Another one of John Browning's famous inventions is the Colt 1911 automatic pistol. This pistol and its successor the 1911A1 still serves the American Army faithfully
Author's Collection

Although highly decorative this Browning Hi-Power is an example of a reliable and strong automatic pistol
Fabrique Nationale

named the pin fire. The solid cartridge sealed the chamber well and the small hole in the side of the case was fairly gas tight. The pin could also be used to extract the cartridge when fired. The main disadvantage was that the cartridge had to be loaded carefully in the correct position so that the pin entered the corresponding slot in the side of the chamber. This ruled out a magazine feed but not a revolver. The most common use therefore of the pin fire was in the multi-shot revolver. The military did not however adopt it in any quantity.

In 1839 a derivation of the patchlock was developed by forming the priming pods into a long tape. This system was patented by an American dentist Edward Maynard. The tape priming system survives today in the child's common cap gun.

The Sharps version of the repeating priming magazine fed a one-eighth inch diameter copper disc containing the priming compound.

The modern rim fire cartridge was developed in 1835 by Flobet who made an equivalent of the modern BB cap. This involved use of the priming agent in the rim of the folded base of the cartridge. The hammer indented the primer by sandwiching the rim of the cartridge between itself and the breech or chamber face. Although the Flobet cartridge was intended primarily for indoor shooting and contained no powder and depended on the priming as a propellant it was not long until the powder was used and cartridges such as the 44 rimfire were invented.

As the American patents office had a fire in 1836 some priceless records were lost which would give documentary evidence of the many attempts and derivations of the above systems. By 1855 Pauly had patented a cartridge with an anvil and primer similar to the modern shotgun cartridge. This was followed in 1866 by the Boxer and Berdan systems. The Boxer system, invented by Colonel Edward Boxer who was a Superintendent of the Laboratory at Woolwich, used a case with a single contro fire hole and a separate primer with a built-in anvil. This leads to easy reloading and has been adopted almost universally in America but not to such an extent in Europe.

Conversely the American Hiram Berdan's cartridge had a dual hole with a built-in anvil and is only used in Europe! The American invention is used in Europe and the British used in America. This illustrates the random way in which inventions developed and were adopted.

The final chapter in the development of the cartridge is possibly the deletion of the case. Caseless ammunition was developed during World War II by the Germans and has been experimented with by most powers since. Weapons such as the Smith &

Wesson submachine gun have been chambered for a caseless 9mm cartridge with an electrically detonated primer.

Perhaps the final development will be the deletion of the propellant in the form that it is now known.

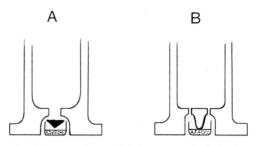

A A boxer primer which features a single flash hole and a primer with a built-in anvil
B A Berdan primer which utilises an anvil integral with the cartridge case, normally two or more flash holes are used

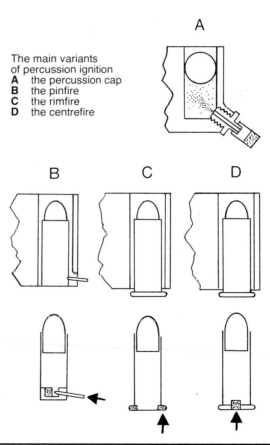

The main variants of percussion ignition
A the percussion cap
B the pinfire
C the rimfire
D the centrefire

Examples of the variety of calibres of pinfire rounds, both ball and blank
Author's Collection

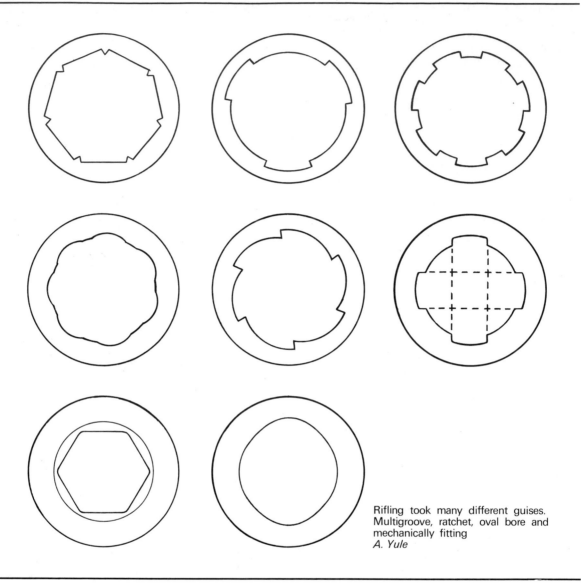

Rifling took many different guises. Multigroove, ratchet, oval bore and mechanically fitting
A. Yule

Chapter 3

Bullets & Rifling

As stones or modified arrows were the first bullets, obviously the early weapons were inefficient as the projectile seldom fitted the bore; but this was of little importance as the gun was more a means of frightening the enemy to death rather than shooting him.

The first manufactured bullets were made from the easiest metal to work with—lead. Moulds could be fashioned from soapstone or even wood and thus the cast ball became the standard projectile. The ball was to last until the 1840s when it was replaced by the elongated bullet.

The actual range of the early firearms was very short indeed as the black powder fouling built up so fast that the barrel either had to be cleaned every few shots or a very undersized ball be used. It was not until the discovery that some form of lubrication was necessary to keep the fouling soft and thus

reduce it that any improvement was made. The lead bullet was in use as early as the 14th century and has continued in one form or another until the present day, although nowadays it is confined to target and sporting shooting as the 'rules of war' have been changed to exclude lead bullets.

The stabilisation of a projectile by spin was known very early on as the flights of arrows and crossbow bolts were angled to promote it. Whether the reasons were fully understood even at a much later date seems doubtful as one of the reasons put forward for the increase in accuracy of the bullet was that devils preferred to ride on a rotating ball rather than on the normal flying one. Perhaps the opposite was the true answer as surely, when the bullet spun, the devils that made it inaccurate fell off, thereby making for accuracy!

As with the gun and gunpowder the inventor of rifling is not known but as he has variously been reported as being named Cotter, Koller, Kotter and Kolner the similarity between the names is obvious and it is, therefore, possible that the inventor did have a similar name.

The definition of rifling is a series of spiral grooves in a gun barrel which impart a spinning motion to the projectile. This, by definition at least, rules out the theory that the first form of rifling was in the form of straight grooves. The reason behind the use of these grooves is attributed by some to hope that the fouling from the powder would accumulate in them rather than in the bore. Accordingly the discovery of the benefit from the spiralling of the grooves would then have occurred accidentally. It is more possible however that the spiralling was a logical follow-on from the flights of the arrow. The probable date of the invention is put as the first half of the 16th century although the first military use was in 1610 by the Danes.

The similarity between the invention of percussion ignition and rifling is that the first application of both was on sporting weapons. Once again this was for the same reason, that what is practical when time can be taken and the target does not shoot back, is not practical on the battlefield.

The types of rifling used vary so much in shape, from multiple curves to heart and crosses, that the author can only presume that some were decorative rather than practical. The practical systems evolved were first tried in serious conflict in the American Civil War when sharp-shooters on both sides used rifled firearms. Notice, however, that the vast majority of the troops still used smooth bore weapons with their inevitable lack of accuracy. The British relied on the massed fire power of a group of troops in formations such as squares which, against the massed armies in Europe and against tribesmen, had been so successful in making up for lack of accuracy with firepower. This, however, was a total failure against fast moving bands of men. Immediately the practice of rifling had become commonplace, forcing the bullet to expand and take the rifling became the main problem especially as the rifling made black powder fouling more acute. More important was the use of undersized balls as small as ·685 for a ·700 bore to ease loading, which defeated the purpose of the rifling. An initial answer was to use an oversized ball and pound it down the barrel. This may have forced the ball into the rifling but needless to say the ball was no longer round and thus at least part of the advantage of the rifling was lost by the deformation.

Among the many methods used to try to cure this trouble were two for use primarily on military weapons and one for sporting or duelling weapons. When time was not at a premium and care could be taken, the turn-off barrel could be used. The turn-off barrel, as its name suggests, has the barrel threaded to the action, allowing a slightly oversized ball to be seated on a counterbored powder chamber. This allowed the barrel to be replaced on the loaded chamber and when the weapon was fired the oversized ball was forced into the rifling.

This system made a very accurate pistol but needless to say speed was not its strong point. The military systems both utilised deformation of the ball

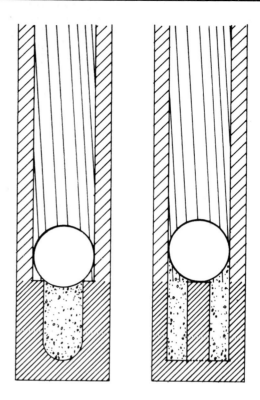

Left: The counter bored powder chamber of Captain Delvigne

Right: The pillar breech of Colonel Thouvenin A. Yule

but in a controlled manner.

The pillar breech (invented by Colonel Thouvenin) incorporated a pillar set in the breech plug (the breech plug was a threaded plug used to close the chamber end of the weapon) round which the powder lay. When the ball was loaded it was forced against the pillar and hammered down thus expanding so that it would take the rifling. A system invented in 1828 by Captain Delvigne deleted the pillar but retained the recessed powder chamber by using a counter bore. The ball was dropped down the barrel until it rested on the counter bore and then it was pounded with the ramrod to expand it into the rifling. All three systems did nothing to alleviate the problem of the black powder fouling. One can only try to imagine the poor soldier having struggled to pound the ball either down the barrel or into the rifling then trying to take a careful aim with tired quivering arms!

The combined problems of fouling and rifling were solved to some degree by the adoption of the patched bullet. This system, although slightly more time-consuming than the undersized ball, did give superb accuracy and minimized fouling. The ball was wrapped in a greased patch which took up the gap between the ball and the rifling thus imparting the spin to the projectile as well as coating the barrel with grease to help keep the fouling soft. Bullets, either mass produced for the military or, for the target shot, the plainsman, or the duellist, were manufactured in one or more round ball bullet moulds. These bullet moulds were always issued with the weapon, enabling the shooter to cast bullets whenever convenient and necessary. The bullet mould, modified with built-in lubricating grooves, is still in use even today with the large number of hand loaders.

The next development which took place was the fitting of the bullet to the rifling, so shaping both the rifling and the bullet. The first experiment was the casting of the bullet with a band on it which fitted the two grooves of the rifling. This purely mechanical type of rifling led to loading problems as any fouling of the grooves made the shaped projectile difficult to load. In 1836 the two groove system was used in small quantities by Britain and named after its inventor—Brunswick. At a later time a ball with two belts at right angles was used with four-groove rifling to suit, but this met with no more success.

Charles Lancaster developed a form of rifling in the shape of an oval. This once again meant the use of a shaped bullet and although it was extremely accurate and met with some use about 1856–1860 it did not last. The other feature of the Lancaster rifling was that it featured a gain twist. The theory being that the bullet would be subjected to less chance of the lead stripping and less strain if the rifling started to spin slowly and then speeded up. This system of slow gain in the rifling has been experimented with continually but has not found general acceptance. The oval bore did however ease the problem of fouling.

In 1860 Whitworth, the inventor of the thread system which bears his name, invented a system of rifling that made absolutely sure that the bullet followed the desired track. He made the bullet and the rifling in the shape of a hexagon. Whitworth rifled weapons were superbly accurate and gained a reputation as an ideal target weapon. However, they did not get the military blessing which was so necessary for commercial success. The use of the modified oval bore in the form of the polygon was also experimented with by Whitworth and although this was successful from the point of accuracy and reduced fouling, the problems of mass production of this shape as with the others of that ilk was to be a decisive factor in its failure. The system has great merit as the firm of Heckler & Koch, after many experiments, have adopted the polygonal rifling in their HK9 pistol, claiming that they have overcome the difficulties of production. They also claim ease of cleaning, additional velocity and less wear as the advantages of their modern polygonally rifled weapon.

An interesting use of the fitted projectile in recent times is in German flare pistols manufactured by Walther during World War II.

By the 1860s various forms of rifling had been tried and many found wanting. The type that found general favour was the multi-groove type whether with three, four, five, six or seven grooves. The depth of the rifling varied from relatively deep to the type used on some weapons today under the name

of micro-groove. The multi-groove rifling in either form is still the standard form of rifling used today with a variety of rates of turn dependent on the type of bullet and its use.

The man who must be given the credit for the adoption, if not the invention of modern rifling is William Metford. His design of a rifled breech loader which was adopted by the British army in 1871 used a paper patched bullet which had the paper wrapping to give the necessary grip between the bullet and shallow seven groove rifling. When the Government decided in 1888 to adopt the ·303 he was called upon to advise. The five groove Enfield rifling which was adopted with the advent of cordite was based on ideas which had been put forward by Metford some years earlier.

The final solution to the problem of the bullet and the rifling was solved when the breech loader was brought into use. This allowed a tight fitting ball or bullet to be used and thus shape itself to the rifling as it was propelled down the barrel. Although the round ball was so poor ballistically that the effective range was in the region of two hundred yards, this is not to say that carefully loaded rifled weapons were not capable of much better performance. The man who brought accuracy to the soldier's rifle was Captain Minié who used a cylindro-conoidal bullet with a hollow base and an expander. The first bullets that Minié used were undersized to make them easy to load even when the barrel was badly fouled. To make the bullet expand and take the rifling it was cast with a hollow base in which an iron plug was fitted. When the weapon was fired the iron plug was driven into the hollow base thus expanding it into the rifling. Developers of the Minié system used wooden plugs or even clay.

Finally it was discovered that the large hollow base would expand without any plug. Minié's work was paralleled, if not preceded, in England by William Greener who designed a bullet with a hollow base and a tapered expander plug.

An interesting form of the combination of the smooth bore and the rifled weapon was the Paradox which had the first three-quarters of the barrel smooth and the last part rifled. The idea being that, with the massive bore sizes used, the recoil of a fully rifled weapon would be too great, but if only the last part of the barrel was rifled this would provide the accuracy and lack of recoil required.

One trend that went step by step with the gradual development of the more efficient weapon was the gradual reduction in the bore size and weight of projectile. This trend continued until the present time as the American forces are now equipped with a weapon of only ·223in bore and sporting rifles use as small as ·17in compared with ·80in of some smooth bore weapons. The reduction of the bore size went hand in hand with the increase in the muzzle velocity of the bullet which in turn made the lead bullet no longer the ideal. The lead could not stand up to the heat and strain of the high velocities and thus a covering of some sort was necessary. This usually consisted of a gilding metal jacket over a lead core but sometimes the core material varied for specific application i.e. the hardened steel core for armour piercing. Other materials have been used

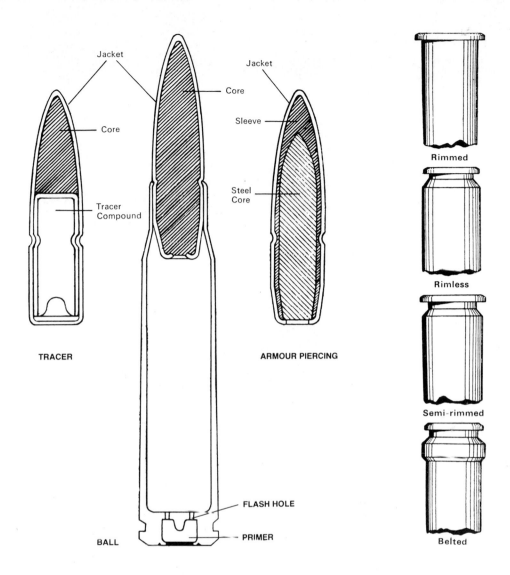

Jacket

Core

Core

Tracer
Compound

TRACER

Core

Jacket

Sleeve

Steel
Core

ARMOUR PIERCING

FLASH HOLE

PRIMER

BALL

Rimmed

Rimless

Semi-rimmed

Belted

The Cartridge. The three basic functions, left, tracer; centre, ball; right, armour piercing.
The method of seating the cartridge in the correct position (head space) is achieved by different
means often at the cartridge base

for the jacket, during wartime shortages, bullets of steel or a solid sintered iron were used.

The effectiveness of the bullet to carry out its task is mainly a function of the weight and the velocity with, to a small extent, the shape and material. The slow moving heavy ball of soft lead was a formidable bullet but it has been established that the small bore ultra-high velocity jacketed bullet does damage out of all proportion to its size and weight. This means a larger number of rounds can be carried and the weapon itself can be lighter in construction. The sacrifices that have to be made are those of long range accuracy and the ability to buck the wind or penetrate bushes etc. The ideal calibre for military weapons had been worked out as 7mm leading to a number of test cartridges of that calibre, all of which were dropped for the 7·62mm NATO round. The Communist Bloc all use the 7·62mm calibre although in a short case. The ideal therefore is still to be found and one can only wonder what will be the outcome of the conflict between the 7·62mm NATO and the ·223in American cartridge, whether other countries will follow America or go their own way.

A very early attempt to manufacture a weapon to fire more than one shot. A four-barrelled hand-cannon
Winchester Gun Museum

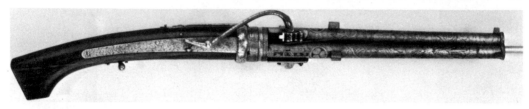

A Japanese matchlock revolver. The three barrels are rotated by hand
Smithsonian Institution

A two-barrel over and under wheellock pistol
Glasgow Art Gallery and Museum

A superimposed load wheellock. This particular
pistol has three separate locks
Glasgow Art Gallery and Museum

Chapter 4

The Multi-Shot Weapon

From the time of the invention of the firearm, man
has attempted to fire more than the one shot in
succession. The results range from the double
barrelled shotgun for the sportman through the
revolver for the cowboy to the automatic rifle for the
modern soldier. The methods of achieving this
range from the highly fanciful to the modern
multi-barrelled American mini gun which fires
10,000 rounds per minute. When it is considered
that in the First World War it took 5000 rounds to kill

one man and in the Second World War 10,000
rounds, the requirement for a multi-fire weapon is
obvious.

The basic types of multi-fire weapon can be
classified as follows: superimposed load; multi-
barrel; revolver; magazine fed and self loading.
As with any attempted clarification system a number
of types inevitably fall between two categories.
The first attempt to improve on the one chance the
marksman had was probably the loading of more
than one projectile into the barrel. This, naturally

enough, did have the desired effect as the bullets spread as they left the barrel and thus improved the chance of a hit on at least one adversary.

The Blunderbuss with its characteristic belled mouth was a development of this theory and was much used by the guards on stagecoaches as a means of hitting fast-moving highwaymen.

The modern shotgun uses exactly the same basic idea and also exhibits the same main disadvantage, certainly from a combat point of view, namely that of the relatively short range.

The superimposed load weapons must date almost from the time of the invention of the firearm, as the Chinese multiple fireworks made from bamboo rods used the same basic idea. The simplest system was to load alternate layers of powder and bullets so that when the foremost of the powder charges was ignited from the muzzle, the first bullet was fired. The loose fit of the ball and the barrel allowed the fire to burn back round the next bullet in the line and ignite the charge and fire it. This continued until all were fired. Another method was to use a ball with a hole bored through it so that when it was carefully loaded with the hole concentrically to the barrel the charges were ignited through each succeeding bullet. Both these methods were unreliable and because of the loose fitting ball in the first case and the hole in the bullet in the second, there was a greater loss of power with a resulting loss in velocity and range. Also there was no method of control as,

once the powder was lit, the weapon continued to fire until empty.

The final superimposed weapons used the same system of multiple loads but employed a more controllable, if not more reliable means of igniting the powder. The loads were fired by either match, flintlock or percussion means, one at a time. In its simplest form the system employed a row of touch holes down the top of the barrel, in theory connecting with the appropriate powder charges. The ignition source was arranged so that it could be moved along the barrel and fire each charge in turn. This system is typified basically in the matchlock and in its most sophisticated form in the highly advanced and well made flint and percussion weapons which had sliding locks which automatically aligned to the appropriate position. This type of arrangement was used in 1818 by Jennings and at about the same time by Henry Mortimer. The drawbacks of this system were that the powder and bullet had to be most carefully loaded otherwise the powder would not be opposite the touch hole. The danger of a misfire of one of the loads or the attempt to fire two bullets at the same time by igniting the wrong touch hole was very real as was also the danger of a multiple discharge if any connection was made between the charge. The next form of multi-shot weapon utilised multiple barrels, the earliest of which date from the second half of the 14th century. The simplest form was a

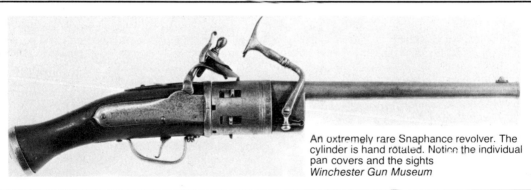

An extremely rare Snaphance revolver. The cylinder is hand rotated. Notice the individual pan covers and the sights
Winchester Gun Museum

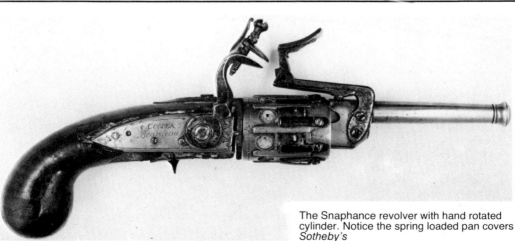

The Snaphance revolver with hand rotated cylinder. Notice the spring loaded pan covers
Sotheby's

row of cannon either ignited one after the other or by a common powder train. The effect of 20 or 30 barrels firing almost simultaneously can be imagined but the prime disadvantage was that, when the weapon had been fired, the time taken to reload each barrel individually was, to say the least, a danger to the gunner. The first weapon that gave some control was the superimposed layer type of multiple barrel weapon where the separate layers of cannon ignition could be fired. This at least allowed the gunner to reload with a reserve of fire power.

In 1411 the Burgundians were equipped with as many as 2000 multiple barrelled weapons which were mobile to a degree. This was surely the forerunner of the Machine Gun Corps!

Pistols were also made with three to seven barrels in France about 1435 but the weight involved must have been a disadvantage when aiming.

The sportsmen soon took up this type of weapon and a number of multi-barrelled sporting guns were made specially for the wild fowler. Many of these weapons had seven barrels, not because it was a magic number but because of the mechanical fact that they were all the same size and so six fitted round one to make the weapon. The weight of such a weapon can only be imagined as the hunter swung his gun after the fowl.

The American Civil War saw the use of two multi-barrel volley guns—the Requa and the Vandenberg. The Requa was maufactured by Billinghurst and had 25 barrels ignited by a powder train which was fired by a percussion cap. This weapon along with the 85 to 100 barrelled Vandenberg was very effective when used to defend the narrow approaches of bridges and the like, as the rain of fire they gave was ideal to stop the storming by massed troops of this type of target. The prime problem still remained; the loading of such a large number of barrels took so much time.

The British fighting on men-of-war at sea had the problem of dealing with the snipers in the fighting tops of the enemy ships who were positioned to kill the enemy officers on deck. (Lord Nelson was killed in this way). The problem of shooting one man with one shot from a swaying top position of a mast whilst he in turn swayed, called for the use of a spread of bullets. As the blunderbuss had not the range, a weapon invented by Captain John Wilson and manufactured by the famous gunmaker Henry Knock was adopted in 1780. This weapon is a magnificently constructed seven-barrelled flintlock which although very unwieldy gave the marksman a chance of success if the flash of ignition did not set the rigging on fire.

The Ducksfoot flintlock pistol was an attempt to provide the ability to fire a spread of bullets. The barrels, which were connected to a common flintlock lock and thus fired together, were spread out in the form of a duck's foot. This gave a thirty or more degree of fire and must have given any man facing such a weapon pause for thought! The Americans continued to use the multi-barrel pistol with the adoption of the double-barrelled Derringer type of pistol such as the Remington, 150,000 of which were produced between 1866 and 1935, and the four barrelled Sharps. These weapons, which have moving firing pins, are like the British Lancaster crossbred weapons.

The double-barrelled shotgun of today with the drilling is a reminder of the multi-barrelled weapon of these early times.

The revolver as a means of firing a repeated shot was first thought of in the 15th century when illustrations show weapons resembling wagon wheels with their axle horizontal and barrels in place of the spokes. These weapons were of cannon ignition and the barrels were revolved by hand. This was an improvement as the firer could continue to shoot at the same target time after time. It is certain that by 1550 the Venice Arsenal had a matchlock revolver. The definition of a true revolver is generally accepted to be a weapon with a stationary barrel and a revolving cylinder. However, all forms of revolving weapon will be grouped under this heading.

The development of the revolver was carried out in separate and distinct stages. The first, as described above, was the hand revolver and indexed barrels with separate firing mechanism for each barrel or cylinder. The deletion of the separate system for each cylinder was perfected with the invention of the percussion lock so that the cylinder, although being

A double barrelled percussion Miquelet lock pistol. The decoration is extremely ornate
Wallis & Wallis

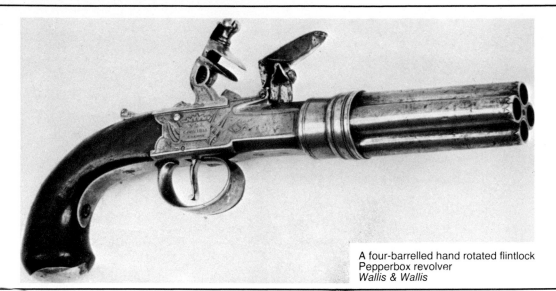

A four-barrelled hand rotated flintlock
Pepperbox revolver
Wallis & Wallis

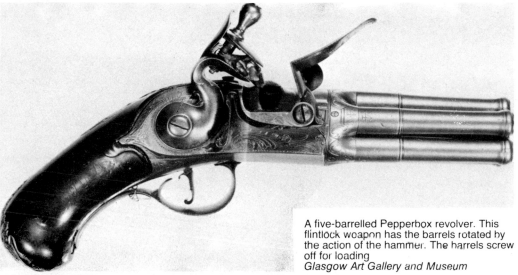

A five-barrelled Pepperbox revolver. This
flintlock weapon has the barrels rotated by
the action of the hammer. The barrels screw
off for loading
Glasgow Art Gallery and Museum

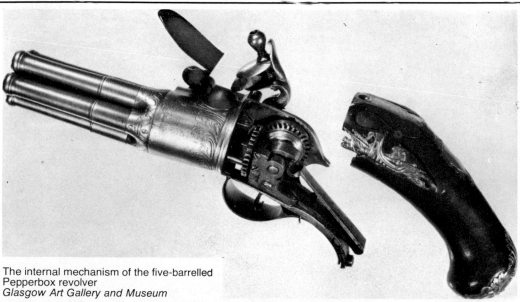

The internal mechanism of the five-barrelled
Pepperbox revolver
Glasgow Art Gallery and Museum

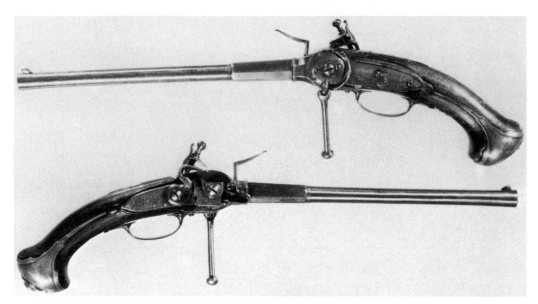

A pair of Lorenzoni system pistols. Movement of the lever in one direction fed powder from the butt magazine and in the other direction a projectile from a similarly placed magazine
Birmingham Art Gallery and Museum

An interesting Belgian 10mm bore gravity fed repeating pistol
Wallis & Wallis

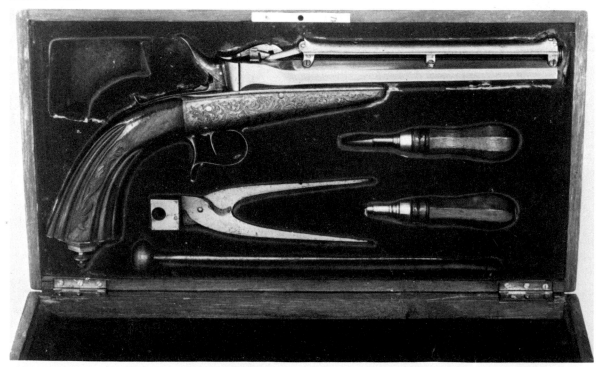

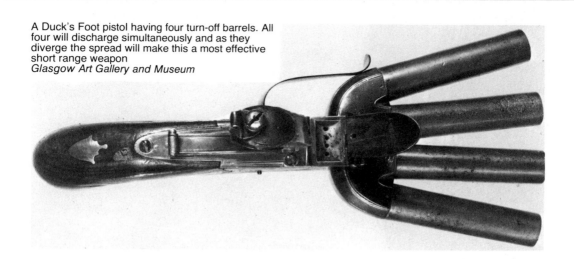

A Duck's Foot pistol having four turn-off barrels. All four will discharge simultaneously and as they diverge the spread will make this a most effective short range weapon
Glasgow Art Gallery and Museum

Bottom: A flintlock turn off barrel Pepperbox revolver. The barrels are hand rotated and the pistol is fitted with a safety catch
Top: A very similar type of pistol which has been converted from flintlock to percussion
Wallis & Wallis

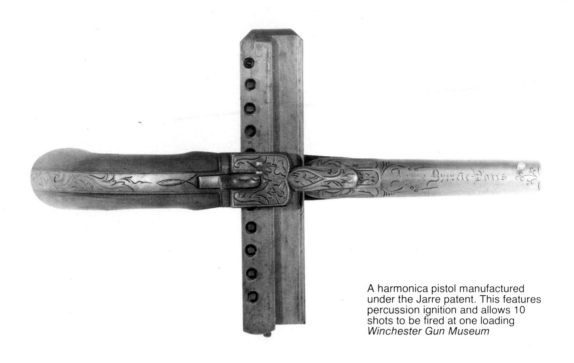

A harmonica pistol manufactured under the Jarre patent. This features percussion ignition and allows 10 shots to be fired at one loading *Winchester Gun Museum*

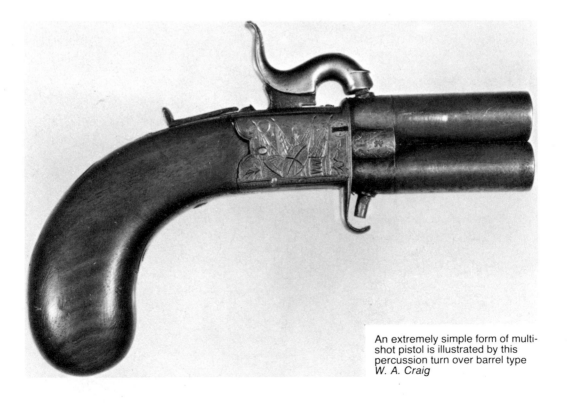

An extremely simple form of multi-shot pistol is illustrated by this percussion turn over barrel type *W. A. Craig*

hand rotated, did not have the encumbrance of a separate lock. The final perfection was the moving and indexing of the cylinder by the movement of the trigger.

The simplest form of the revolver is illustrated by the turnover barrel pistol, although it has only two barrels and these have to be turned by hand. The means of ignition varied from two complete flintlocks on the earlier weapons to the simplest single hammer of the percussion era.

The hand revolved barrels developed through the 16th and 17th centuries with the wheellock, then to the Snaphance and flintlock pepper boxes. Henry Knock had a development of his volley gun, late 1780s, with hand revolved barrels. In 1718 the forerunner of the revolving barrelled machine gun was invented by James Puckle. This flintlock weapon had hand-indexed cylinders with the addition of a gas seal operated by winding the rear of the breech forward for each shot. The truly remarkable feature of this weapon was the designed intention of firing round bullets at the easy-to-kill Christians and square for the very difficult-to-kill Infidels. This design problem would daunt the modern gun designer, far less the unsophisticated gunsmiths of that time.

The revolver then had cylinders which revolved not only as the type known today, but with wheels of radially drilled chambers either set vertically or horizontally. These failed because of the bulk of the weapon. In 1851 a Mr Porter patented the vertical type and in 1837 a Mr J. Cochran the horizontal one.

The actual inventor of the modern self-revolving and self-indexing weapon has often been named as Samuel Colt who, when on a sailing ship saw the wheel revolving and thus designed the first revolver on the spot. This is dated about 1835 but, as many multi-barrelled pepper boxes with hand rotated barrels were in use and these only lacked the vital revolving mechanism, it is therefore logical that many attempts were made to perfect them. This leads one to suppose that the invention was made before Colt. What must be said of Samuel Colt was that his pistols led the way to the development of

the revolver as a practical military weapon and accelerated the achievements of today's perfection. The rifle also became a revolver when Colt and Smith & Wesson made versions respectively. The weapons were not a success, as the vastly more practical Henry and Winchester lever action weapons came on the scene.

Colt's revolvers were single action, that is to say they required the hammer to be cocked for each shot. In 1851 Robert Adam perfected the double action revolver, thus leading to a higher rate of fire. A final derivation was the recoil-operated revolver, the Webley-Fosbery which was invented in 1901. The cylinder on this weapon was revolved by the action of the recoil thus making a form of automatic revolver.

In 1862 Gatling took out a patent for a revolving-barrelled machine gun that revolutionised the theory of fire-power and should have superseded the ranks of men equipped with single shot weapons and the volley gun. This weapon and its successors were not, however, to be recognised until the First World War when the Germans recognised their worth. It is said that Custer's Last Stand need never have happened as he could have taken a Gatling gun with him! He, however, dismissed it as a waste of the carrying capacity of his troops and thus died from the massed assault of the Red Indians.

The revolver is still the official side arm of some countries today although it has largely been superseded by the automatic pistol. The Gatling gun still is, with the modern electrically driven derivative, in front line service both in aircraft and in helicopters. A derivation of the Gatling type of system uses one barrel but a revolving feed system. An example of this type is the Aden cannon.

The magazine in its first form was a two-part system developed by Kalthoff with the powder held in one part and the bullets in another. The ball magazine under the barrel would be no worry but the powder in the stock with the ever present danger of a detonation must have been a hazard. The relative components were fed by the rotation of a lever that allowed a charge of powder into the chamber along

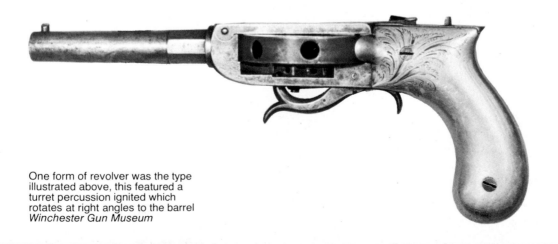

One form of revolver was the type illustrated above, this featured a turret percussion ignited which rotates at right angles to the barrel
Winchester Gun Museum

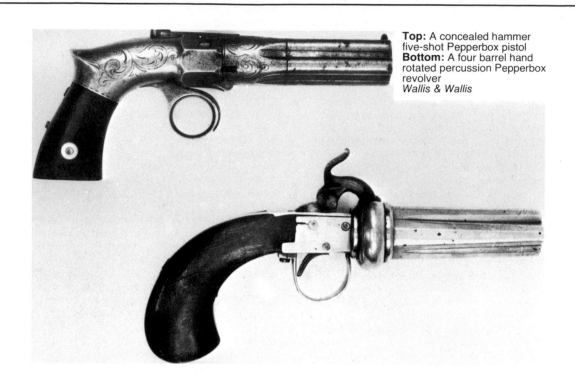

Top: A concealed hammer five-shot Pepperbox pistol
Bottom: A four barrel hand rotated percussion Pepperbox revolver
Wallis & Wallis

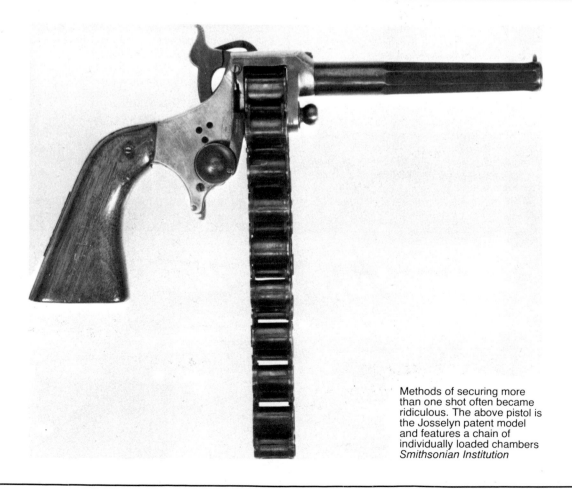

Methods of securing more than one shot often became ridiculous. The above pistol is the Josselyn patent model and features a chain of individually loaded chambers
Smithsonian Institution

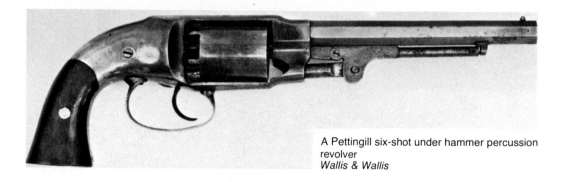

A Pettingill six-shot under hammer percussion revolver
Wallis & Wallis

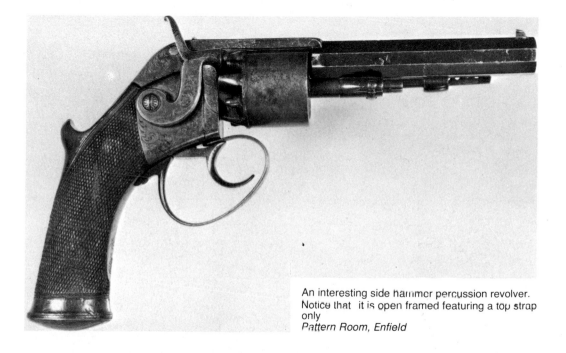

An interesting side hammer percussion revolver. Notice that it is open framed featuring a top strap only
Pattern Room, Enfield

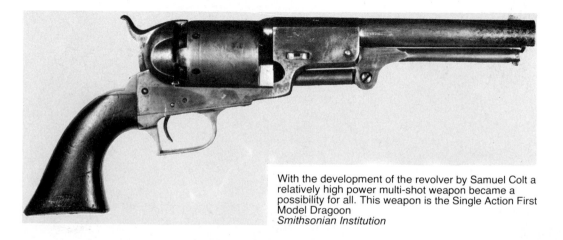

With the development of the revolver by Samuel Colt a relatively high power multi-shot weapon became a possibility for all. This weapon is the Single Action First Model Dragoon
Smithsonian Institution

A Colt revolver with cast
silver grips and intricate
engraving
Christies

An interesting two barrel multi-
chambered revolver. Two
shots are fired at each pull of
the trigger
Pattern Room, Enfield

The standard service sidearm of the British Army was for a long time the ·38 Service Revolver. The upper pistol No.2 MkI* has the hammer spur removed so that it can only be fired double-action. The bottom pistol is a cutaway demonstration model featuring the standard hammer
J. Bowman

with the ball. In about 1640 along with Kalthoff, Lorenzoni also developed the same system but had both the powder and the balls on the butt.

These systems and others of this type failed because of the fouling which took place and which led to the mechanism becoming jammed. The Harmonica gun with its sliding chambers was probably the nearest to a magazine weapon. The slide which moved across the breech was, however, too unwieldy for success.

The invention in 1848 of the combined bullet and powder by Hunt for the Volition repeater made the magazine a practical possibility. The Volcanic pistols and rifles used a magazine tube under the barrel.

This development was closely followed by both Henry in 1862 and Winchester in 1866. The tube magazine was also used on the Vettereli bolt action rifle and on the first of the Mauser designs. In 1879 James Lee invented the box magazine that was to remain the standard method of feeding. In 1885 Mannlicher developed the clip which could hold the cartridges ready to load into the box magazine. There are two types of box magazine, the single column containing the cartridges in a single line and the dual column which has the cartridges in two lines driven upward by, in some cases, a roller follower. The last form of magazine to be developed but the one that is perhaps best known because of the Thompson submachine gun is the drum.

The two main types of drum are the horizontal feed and the vertical feed. In the horizontal feed typified by the Lewis gun drum, the cartridges are stored in a radial fashion with the point of the bullet towards the centre. The cartridges are fed downwards into the weapon as the drum revolves. The Thompson type of drum magazine has the cartridges stored with their axis parallel to that of the drum. The cartridges are forced by a spring-driven follower to follow a spiral track into the weapon. German machine guns of the Second World War were sometimes fitted with a double drum of this type. The prime advantage of the drum magazine over the box is the extra capacity of up to 100 rounds as opposed to 20 or 30. The problems are the resultant weight and unreliable feed. Weapons such as the Italian Breda machine gun utilised a strip or tray feed. The cartridges were held in place on the tray by clips and were even on some types of weapons replaced when empty. A severe disadvantage was that the tray could gather any dirt or be damaged and thus could become unreliable.

The final stage in the feed system was the belt which initially was made of canvas but has been developed into metal link of either the disintegrating or non-disintegrating types. The main advantage of the belt is that the gun can be fired almost without pause, the belts being joined while the weapn is in use. Also the belts of ammunition can be distributed among the members of the platoon.

The self-loading weapon completed the development of the multiple-shot weapon. From 1881 to 1883 Hiram Maxim experimented with a Winchester, using the recoil to operate a lever to move the action. In 1893 he developed the short stock gas pistol followed in 1885 by a short recoil weapon with a locked breech developed by Von Mannlicher. The development was rapid, with such

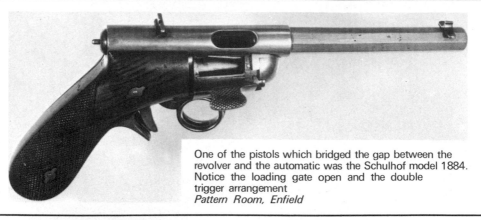

One of the pistols which bridged the gap between the revolver and the automatic was the Schulhof model 1884. Notice the loading gate open and the double trigger arrangement
Pattern Room, Enfield

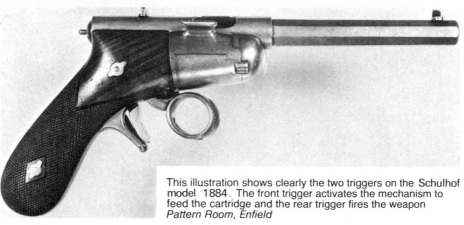

This illustration shows clearly the two triggers on the Schulhof model 1884. The front trigger activates the mechanism to feed the cartridge and the rear trigger fires the weapon
Pattern Room, Enfield

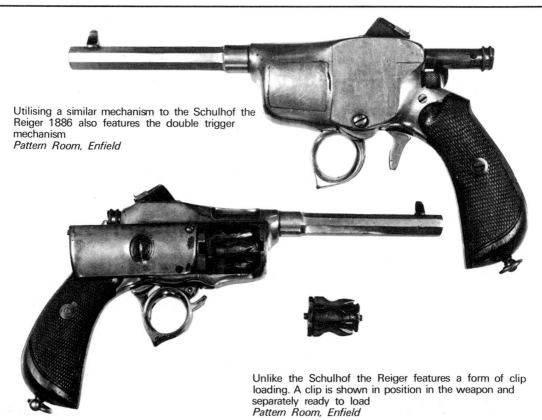

Utilising a similar mechanism to the Schulhof the Reiger 1886 also features the double trigger mechanism
Pattern Room, Enfield

Unlike the Schulhof the Reiger features a form of clip loading. A clip is shown in position in the weapon and separately ready to load
Pattern Room, Enfield

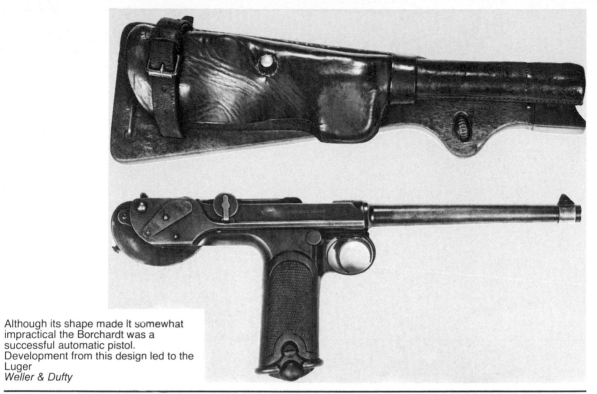

Although its shape made it somewhat
impractical the Borchardt was a
successful automatic pistol.
Development from this design led to the
Luger
Weller & Dufty

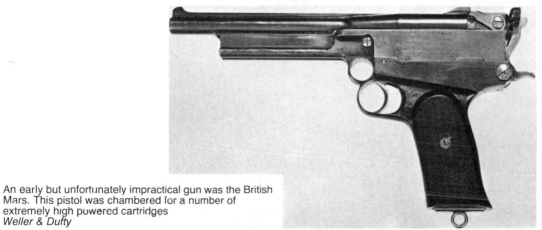

An early but unfortunately impractical gun was the British
Mars. This pistol was chambered for a number of
extremely high powered cartridges
Weller & Dufty

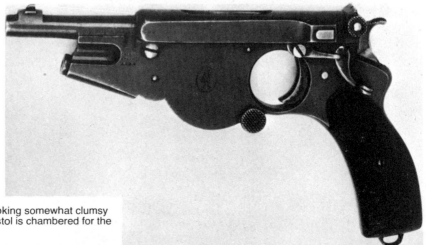

The Bergman design although looking somewhat clumsy
was relatively successful. This pistol is chambered for the
5mm Bergmann cartridge
Wallis & Wallis

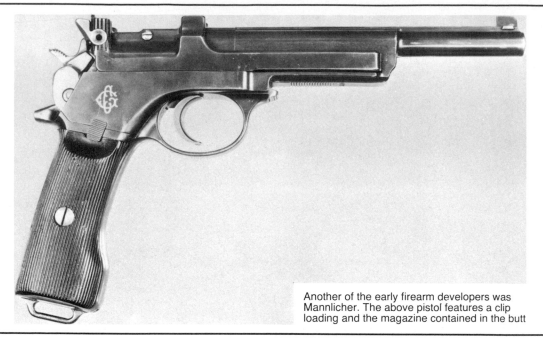

Another of the early firearm developers was Mannlicher. The above pistol features a clip loading and the magazine contained in the butt

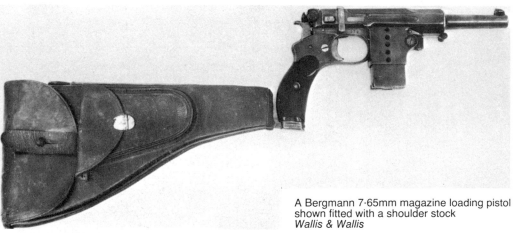

A Bergmann 7·65mm magazine loading pistol shown fitted with a shoulder stock
Wallis & Wallis

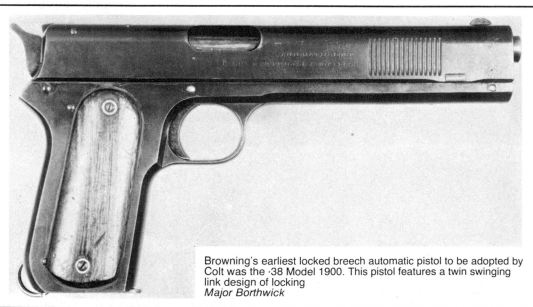

Browning's earliest locked breech automatic pistol to be adopted by Colt was the ·38 Model 1900. This pistol features a twin swinging link design of locking
Major Borthwick

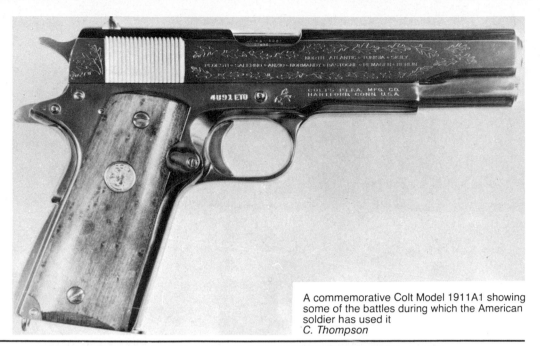

A commemorative Colt Model 1911A1 showing some of the battles during which the American soldier has used it
C. Thompson

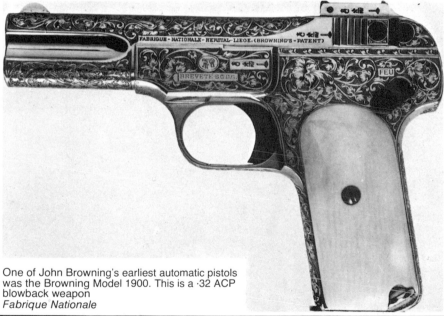

One of John Browning's earliest automatic pistols was the Browning Model 1900. This is a ·32 ACP blowback weapon
Fabrique Nationale

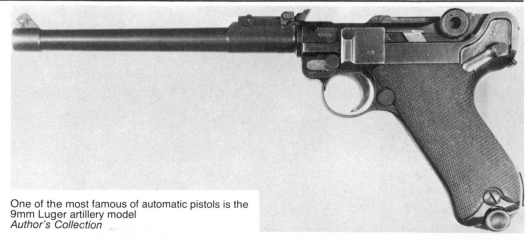

One of the most famous of automatic pistols is the 9mm Luger artillery model
Author's Collection

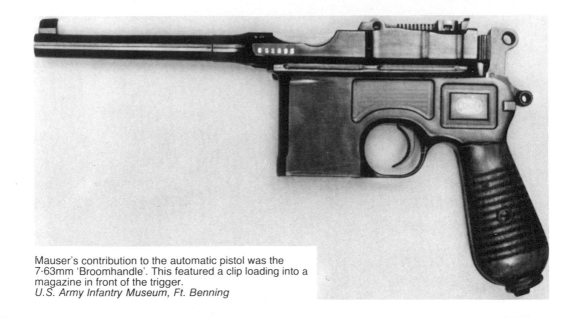

Mauser's contribution to the automatic pistol was the
7·63mm 'Broomhandle'. This featured a clip loading into a
magazine in front of the trigger.
U.S. Army Infantry Museum, Ft. Benning

A SIG P210 De Luxe finish pistol. This uses the Petters
patent and has the reputation of being one of the world's
finest and strongest automatic pistols
SIG

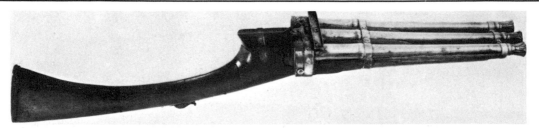

An Indian three-barrelled matchlock weapon.
Notice the primitive sights and the large pan which
would ignite all three charges almost
simultaneously
Crown Copyright, Tower of London

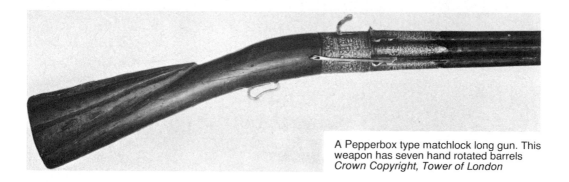

A Pepperbox type matchlock long gun. This
weapon has seven hand rotated barrels
Crown Copyright, Tower of London

A rotating chamber flintlock. This weapon has a
single barrel and the two chambers have a
complete pan and frizzen mechanism
Glasgow Art Gallery and Museum

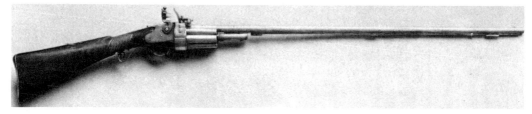

The Wheeler flintlock revolving rifle of 1820
Smithsonian Institution

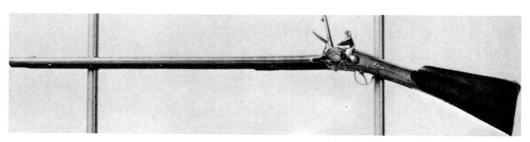

A Lorenzoni system repeating flintlock
Smithsonian Institution

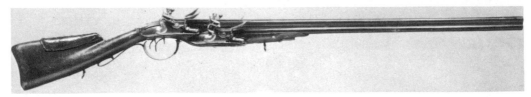

A four-barrelled long gun which features four
complete flint locks
Glasgow Art Gallery and Museum

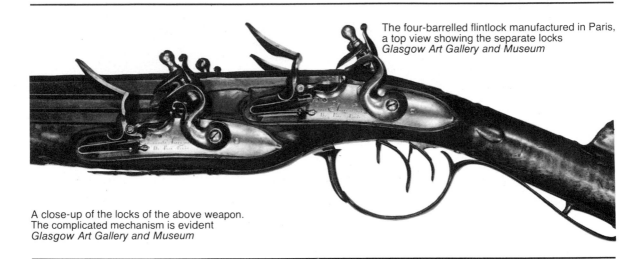

The four-barrelled flintlock manufactured in Paris,
a top view showing the separate locks
Glasgow Art Gallery and Museum

A close-up of the locks of the above weapon.
The complicated mechanism is evident
Glasgow Art Gallery and Museum

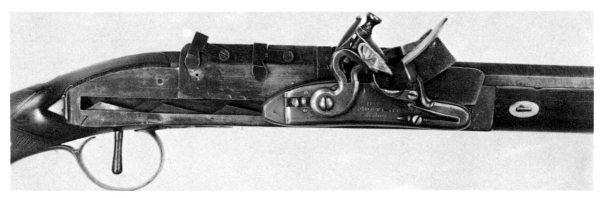

A superimposed load flintlock long gun manufactured by Mortimer. The lock
was slid backwards to fire each of the charges in turn
Winchester Gun Museum

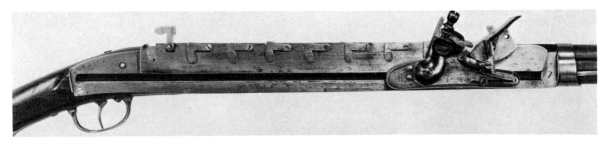

A North 10-shot superimposed load flintlock long gun. As can be seen from
the lock this was manufactured in 1825
Winchester Gun Museum

A Pennsylvanian long rifle with turn over barrel
Smithsonian Institution

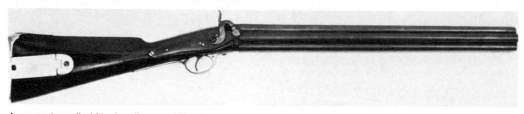

A seven-barrelled Nock volley gun. This is
percussion fired
Wallis & Wallis

A Haviland & Bennett patent model revolving
chamber rifle. Notice that the chambers revolve at
right angles to the barrel axis
Smithsonian Institution

A Porter repeating rifle. This is the patent model dated 1851. Notice the complicated turret mechanism
Smithsonian Institution

Paul Mauser brought the modern bolt action rifle into the armies across the world. The top rifle is an 1889
model and the bottom a modified version of same. Both of these rifles were manufactured for the Belgian
army by Fabrique Nationale
Fabrique Nationale

The straight pull bolt found favour with some manufacturers. The above is a K43 manufactured by SIG
SIG

The post World War II automatic rifle is typified by the FN Model 1950. This was used in Korea by the Belgian troops
Fabrique Nationale

A typical example of the modern 5·56mm selectable fire rifle is the Armalite AR18. The above version is fitted with a telescopic sight
Armalite Inc.

The hand operated machine gun reached a state of perfection with the later model of the Gatling. The weapon is shown here with its trolley tripod and spare ammunition boxes
Birmingham Art Gallery & Museum

The early attempt at the machine gun was the Puckle gun. This was flintlock ignited and featured the useful solution to kill people of different races in that it fired round bullets to kill Christians and square to kill Infidels
Crown Copyright, Tower of London

John Browning was one of the first of the designers to perfect the machine gun. Shown here is a prototype of 1895
Browning

An example of the latest design of General Purpose Machine Gun is the SIG. It is shown here on its tripod fitted with infra red sighting gear
SIG

The Villar Perosa is often credited as the first submachine gun. The above weapon is shown on its bipod
Pattern Room, Enfield

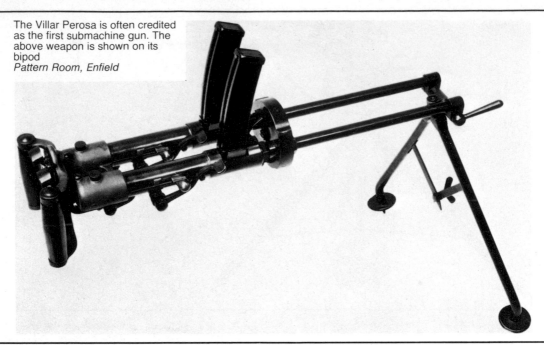

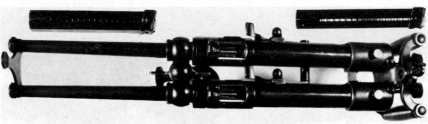

The twin barrells, the feed, the cocking handle and triggers of the Villar Perosa are clearly visible in this view
Pattern Room Enfield

One of the most famous submachine guns is the Thompson. The weapon shown here is a Model 1928.
It is fitted with a box magazine and a Cutts compensator
Smithsonian Institution

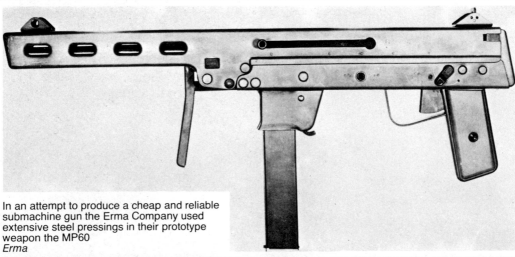

In an attempt to produce a cheap and reliable submachine gun the Erma Company used extensive steel pressings in their prototype weapon the MP60
Erma

Utilising all the latest techniques and design the Ingram M11 submachine gun is an example of how compact the weapon can be. This weapon is fitted with a silencer which is extremely effective
Pattern Room, Enfield

The alternative feeds for the Thompson submachine gun are a 20 round box magazine the 50 round drum and the 100 round drum
Pattern Room, Enfield

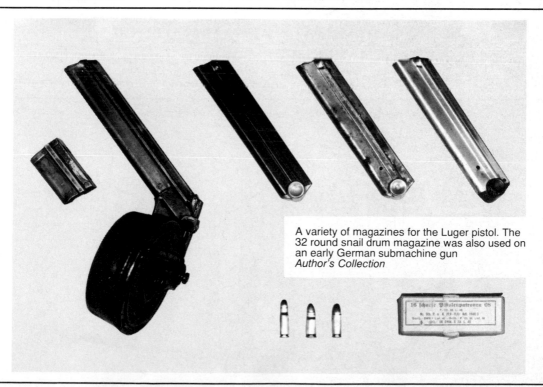

A variety of magazines for the Luger pistol. The 32 round snail drum magazine was also used on an early German submachine gun
Author's Collection

The Italian Breda machine gun utilises the clip feed. This has the doubtful advantage of having the empty cases replaced in the clip as the weapon fires
Lowland Brigade Depot

The most popular feed for the machine gun is the belt feed. The type shown here is for the Vickers machine gun
Lowland Brigade Depot

The almost standard method for feeding a pistol is the box magazine inserted in the butt
Author's Collection

◀ A German belt-loader in operation. The belt is a non-disintegrating link type
Imperial War Museum

A typical example of the cartridge clip. This is for the Russian 7.62 short cartridge
Author's Collection

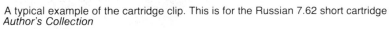

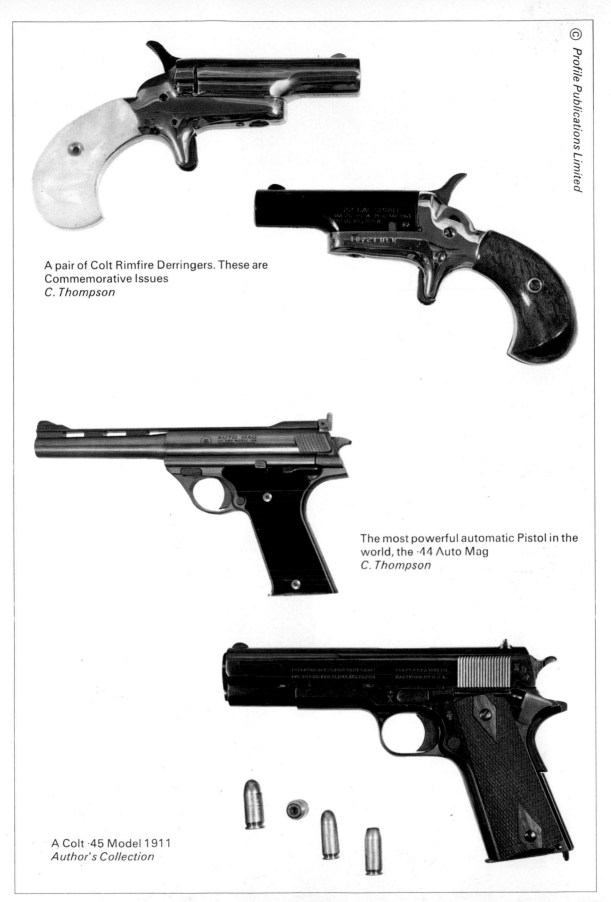

A pair of Colt Rimfire Derringers. These are
Commemorative Issues
C. Thompson

The most powerful automatic Pistol in the
world, the ·44 Auto Mag
C. Thompson

A Colt ·45 Model 1911
Author's Collection

A Colt Single Action Army
C. Thompson

An Enfield ·38 Revolver Demonstration
Model
J. Bowman

A SIG 7·62 Service Rifle. Notice the Bipod and Grenade Launcher on the Barrel.
Pattern Room Enfield

An Artillery Luger with an 8in Barrel
Author's Collection

A Browning Hi-Power with Factory Engraving
C. Thompson

Prideux Loaders
Author's Collection

A Powder Flask made of brass and in the
shape of a pineapple
Author's Collection

A Swiss Schmidt Rubin Straight Pull Bolt
Action Rifle
Lowland Brigade Depot

The Lock from a Flintlock Blunderbuss
Andrew Youle

A Lancaster two barrelled pistol. Compare with four barrelled version opposite

A Lancaster four-barrel pistol. This is an example of a standing breech with a hinged frame. The weapon is fired by a rotating striker
Pattern Room, Enfield

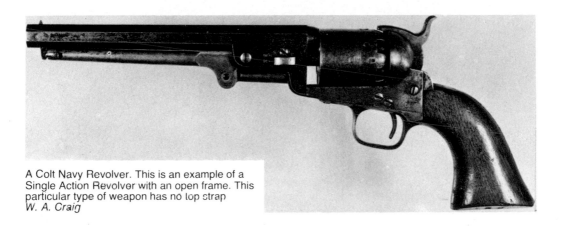

A Colt Navy Revolver. This is an example of a Single Action Revolver with an open frame. This particular type of weapon has no top strap
W. A. Craig

Chapter 5

The Action

To provide any form of repetitive fire, other than that provided by the use of multiple cannon ignition, a system or method of operation is required to allow a cartridge to be loaded with speed and ease.

There are four methods of operation: mechanical, blowback, recoil, and gas, or a combination of one or more of these.

The primer must be detonated by some means and this is dependent on the type of action employed but is of either hammer fire or striker fire. The hammer fired type is self-descriptive in that the firing pin is either integral with or hit by a hammer and thus the cartridge is fired. A subdivision is the concealed type of hammer, where the hammer is contained in the weapon. The striker fired weapon has no hammer and the firing pin itself is the means of firing the weapon. This type is also called hammerless.

Mechanical Action

The single shot weapon, be it rifle or pistol, illustrates all the basic principles, namely standing breeches, rising block, falling block, rolling block and rotating bolt. These all require the firer to load the live round and eject the fired case from the weapon. In fact, most automatic weapons use one or more of these basic actions in a modified form.

Standing Breech Hinged Frame

The standing breech weapons use a hinged frame in a similar manner to the modern shotgun. The breech lock is operated by means of a lever, trigger guard or in some revolvers a form of lift or squeeze catch. When the breech is unlocked the barrel can then be hinged down, or, less commonly, to the side, or up for loading. The Derringer No 3 is a typical example of the side swing single shot. Another weapon of this type is the M60 grenade launcher.

The Revolver

The revolver is an example of the standing breech type of weapon and as such is made in two types—solid or hinged frame with the action being divided into single, double or automatic.

SINGLE ACTION

The single action revolver is one in which the user must cock the weapon for each shot. The action of the hammer being pulled back moves the cylinder round to align the chamber to be fired and also causes it to be indexed accurately. When the trigger is squeezed the hammer falls and the weapon fires; before another shot can be fired the hammer has once again to be pulled back. The cowboy trick of 'fanning' the trigger is accomplished by holding the trigger back and only using the hammer. A 'slip gun' has no trigger and is used purely by the action of the hammer.

DOUBLE ACTION

Double action requires the trigger mechanism to carry out the complete cycle of the revolver. When the trigger is pulled the cylinder is revolved, the hammer raised, the cylinder indexed and the hammer allowed to fall. This system by its very nature cannot provide the precise trigger of the single action. For this reason most double action revolvers can also be fired single action with the exception of such weapons as the British ·38 Enfield No 2 Mk I service revolver where the hammer spur is removed.

THE SELF-LOADING REVOLVER

This type of weapon is rare and the best known is the Webley-Fosbery. The Webley-Fosbery uses the recoil of the weapon to slide the cylinder which has zigzag grooves, back along a stud, thus rotating it. This system, although providing an accurate and reliable weapon, was never adopted in any large numbers.

An early Double Action Percussion Revolver of the open frame type. This particular instance the barrel and grip are joined by a top strap. Notice the intricate ramrod
Pattern Room, Enfield

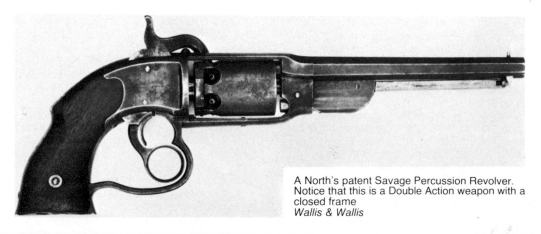

A North's patent Savage Percussion Revolver. Notice that this is a Double Action weapon with a closed frame
Wallis & Wallis

A Mauser Revolver shown with the barrel tipped vertically for loading
Pattern Room, Enfield

A Smith & Wesson Revolver which utilises a swing-out cylinder for loading
Author's Collection

A two-barrelled multi-shot revolver. This is a Double Action weapon and the barrel is shown tipped backwards for loading
Pattern Room, Enfield

Probably the simplest pistol ever mass-produced—the Liberator. Notice that the breech is merely a sliding gate through which the locking pin formed by part of the hammer slides. This is a Single Shot weapon
Lowland Brigade Depot

A Webley Service Revolver. The barrel tips down for loading. This weapon also features automatic extraction

Below: A pin-fire 11mm Degueldre Revolver. Notice that on this weapon the barrel and cylinder move forward from a standing breech for loading
Wallis & Wallis

Top Right: A Webley Fosbery self cocking and indexing revolver, cocked ready to fire
Lowland Brigade Depot
Right: The Webley Fosbery shown in the recoil position and the cylinder half way to being indexed
Lowland Brigade Depot

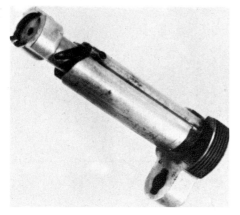

The rotating bolthead from the long recoil from an automatic pistol. Notice the spiral groove which guides the rotating head
Author's Collection

The most powerful automatic pistol—the ·44 AutoMag. This pistol features a rotating bolthead and is of the short recoil type
C. Thompson

SOLID AND OPEN FRAME FIXED CYLINDER

The solid frame revolver has, as the name suggests, no means of breaking for loading. Early open frame revolvers i.e. those without a top strap, also have no means of opening for loading. The loading of revolvers of this type is either accomplished from the front as in the early percussion sort or from the rear as in the cartridge Colts. Ejection of the empty cases must be carried out one by one, therefore this type of weapon is slow to load.

HINGED FRAME MOVING BARREL

The hinged frame moving barrel was made in three basic types; the swing down, the swing up and the swing sideways. The hinged down achieved the largest degree of success with a variety of locking methods for the frame. The system allowed the use of a simultaneous ejection activated by the action of tipping the barrel down. The tip up barrel did not achieve any degree of success but the Mauser pistol illustrated is an example. The final type which was little used is the side swing.

SOLID FRAME SWING CYLINDER

This type of weapon is typified by the Smith & Wesson range and has a crane on which the cylinder is carried. The crane can be unlocked from the frame and the cylinder swung out. The ejector rod can then remove all the empty cases in one movement and fresh rounds can be loaded with ease. The cylinder is locked into place by the ejector rod on the front and a continuation of it at the rear. The Smith & Wesson triple lock had an extra lock at the crane and was the high point in the swing out action revolver.

THE GAS SEAL REVOLVER

The Gas Seal Revolver is typified by the Russian Nagant and is an attempt to remove the small drop in velocity which occurs from the loss of pressure through the gap between the cylinder and the barrel. The Nagant uses an extra long cartridge case which when loaded protrudes from the front of the cylinder. When the trigger is pulled the cylinder is moved forward and the front of the case enters the barrel and seals the gap. The difference in velocity by test with the gas seal and without was small but noticeable.

There have been a number of other revolver designs but all use derivations or combinations of these types.

Rising Block

This little used system employed a breech block which was raised by the action of a lever, allowing the weapon to be loaded. The block slides in two machined slots in the receiver and is raised by levers pivoted on pins. The levers are depressed, the blocks raised and at the same time an extractor removes the empty case. The weapon was either fired by hammer or more rarely a striker incorporated in the breech block.

Falling Block

The original falling block action was invented by Henry Peabody, an American, and used a breech block which is hinged high at the rear so that when the action is opened the block falls down and so clears the chamber for loading. The action is worked from an under lever combined with the trigger guard. The weapon used an external hammer that had to be cocked by hand for each shot and struck a firing pin carried in the falling block. The Swiss, Frederick Martini, modified the action by substituting an internal firing pin mechanism contained in the breech block. This was cocked by the action of the under lever and thus removed the bulky hammer. This action is used in many modern target weapons.

Dropping Block

The dropping block design is one of the basic designs that are still in use today. The dropping block was derived from a number of artillery pieces and weapons of this type. It was also on the first Winchester ·22in rimfire single shot. The design uses a breech block that slides in a vertical direction in slots machined in the receiver walls. The two types of falling block are the 'high' and the 'low wall'. These are descriptions of the length of the slides cut in the receiver wall. The 'low wall' had the slide slots only as high as the bore axis and thus was suited to relatively low powered cartridges only, while the 'high wall' has the slots cut to the top of the receiver and thus has more strength. The weapons are either fired by an external hammer, internal hammer or striker fired.

Rolling Block

The rolling block action is one of the simplest as only two components are needed and one of these is the hammer. The breech block is hinged at its lowest point and is spring loaded so that it stays forward against the breech. A lever is provided to pull it rearward for loading. On the rear face of the block is a surface that can, when the hammer is down, be locked in place by a similar surface on the hammer. The lock is so designed that the surfaces are mated best when the hammer is fully down and striking the firing pin in the block. This lock has been used in a variety of forms but all are a modification of the basic Remington action.

Hinged Breech Block

There are innumerable types of hinged breech blocks but most are variations of either the Snider side hinged block or the Springfield front hinged block. These systems were used in large quantities to convert the muzzle loading weapons to breech loaders.

Bolt Action

The bolt action as its name suggests works in a similar manner to the standard turning bolt as used on a house door. The bolt can be lifted from a locking recess and then slid open. In the weapon the cartridge can then be loaded into the chamber, the bolt is then returned forward and the handle turned down to lock.

The first practical bolt action weapon firing a metallic cartridge is usually ascribed to Paul Mauser of Germany who, with Samuel Norris patented a bolt action weapon in the United States on 2 June 1868. Paul Dreyse had patented a bolt action weapon in

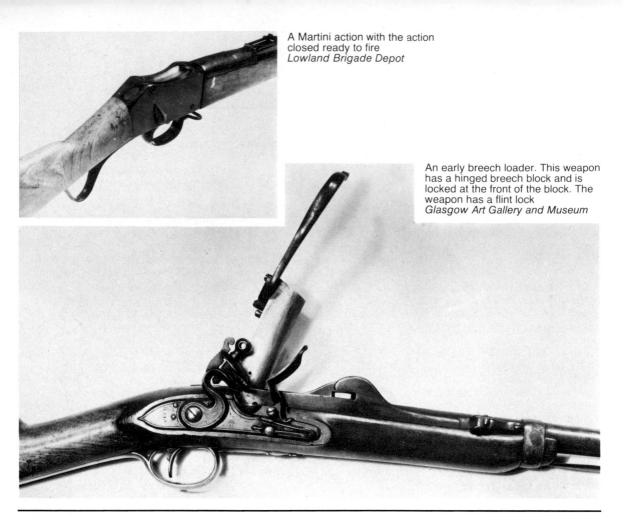

A Martini action with the action
closed ready to fire
Lowland Brigade Depot

An early breech loader. This weapon
has a hinged breech block and is
locked at the front of the block. The
weapon has a flint lock
Glasgow Art Gallery and Museum

A diagram of the Ferguson Rifle showing the method of operation of the screwed breech
United Services Museum

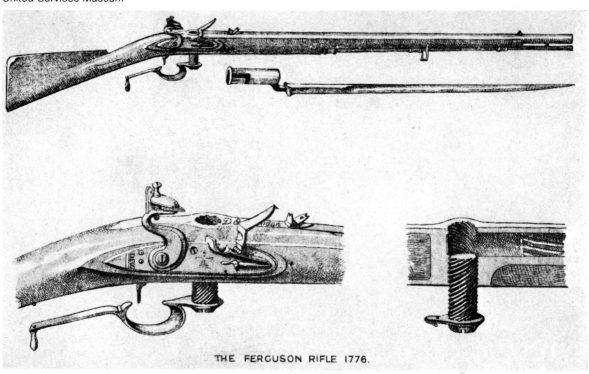

THE FERGUSON RIFLE 1776.

1835 but this was a needle gun. The turn bolt weapon action can be divided into three wide classifications, front locking, rear locking and straight pull. The Mauser turn bolt action utilises locking lugs on the front of the bolt which when the bolt is turned fit into recesses in the receiver ring. The identification of the Mauser type is the use of these front mounted lugs.

The Enfield bolt action utilises locking lugs further back than those of the Mauser although the operation is similar. The use of the locking lugs into the main receiver body give an extremely strong action although the front locking Mauser types are renowned for accuracy. One disadvantage of the rear locking types is the need to cut away part of the body to receive the long lug and thus weaken it. The Mannlicher uses a straight pull type of bolt and all such weapons can be classed as Mannlicher developments. The locking method employed in the first Mannlichers is a block which was pivoted from the rear of the bolt, dropped and wedged down when the bolt was closed. This block abuts against the receiver stopping the rearward movement of the bolt. On the straight rearward pull of the bolt the wedge is withdrawn and the block can move up and allow the bolt to move rearwards. The straight pull action can also work by the use of locking lugs on a turning bolt head which are cammed into recesses in the receiver by the action of the forward movement of the bolt. This type of action was used in the famous Ross rifle which although proving superbly accurate as a civilian weapon did not stand up to the rigours of trench warfare in the First World War.

Lever Action

The first of the rifle actions to use the locked breech and the lever action was the Volition repeater. This used a hand operated lever to eject the fired case and feed a fresh round from a magazine, a tube in the case of the Volcanic and its derivatives, the Henry and the early Winchesters.

Pump Action

The pump action, or as it sometimes called, the Trombone action, utilises a slide under the barrel to operate the cycle by a rearward and forward movement.

Self Loading Actions

In the following types of action the processes of loading and ejecting are carried out by the weapon and not the firer.

Blowback and Blow Forward

Blowback systems are divided into three separate types. The simple blowback, the delayed blowback and the blow forward. The blow forward is very rare owing to its somewhat impractical nature.

BLOW FORWARD

The blow forward system utilises the force of the combustion to blow the barrel group forward, leaving the breech face with the extractor holding the empty case. At the limit of the forward travel an ejector hits the empty case and throws it clear. The rearward motion of the barrel, driven by the recoil spring, picks up a fresh round and chambers it ready for firing. This system has numerous disadvantages, the main one being the difficulty of maintaining a reliable feed. The SIG AK53 utilised this system but was abandoned in favour of a weapon with a more normal type of operation.

BLOWBACK

The blowback system utilises the gas pressure to drive back a breech block. The empty case is forced clear of the chamber by the pressure. On some weapons an extractor claw is attached to the breech block to remove misfires or unfired rounds. The breech block is driven forward by a recoil spring and chambers a fresh round. This system is the most widely used for low powered rimfire sporting weapons such as target pistols and for submachine guns.

The Ferguson screwed breech. This system provided a method of breech loading. The weapon is a Flintlock Rifle
Glasgow Art Gallery and Museum

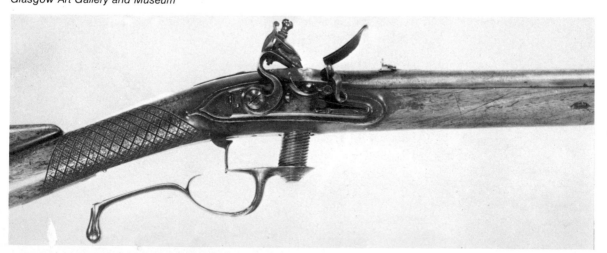

The Westley Richards breech
loader which utilised a paper
cartridge. The weapon is
shown with the breech open
Lowland Brigade Depot

The Snider conversion of the Enfield Musket
features a side hinged block. This weapon is of the
later type with an additional lock controlled by the
knob at the side of the breech block
Lowland Brigade Depot

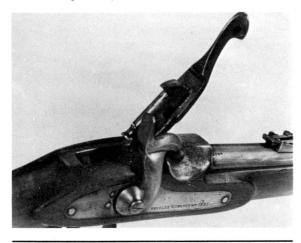

A further form of breech
block is featured on this
rifle. This illustrates it in
the closed position
Lowland Brigade Depot

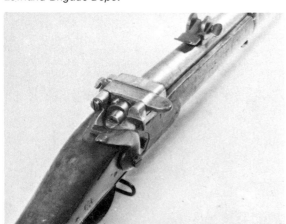

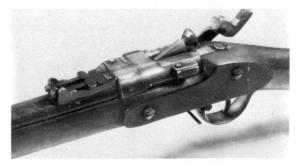

The Snider conversion with the breech block
closed. Notice how this weapon is neatly
converted to percussion fire by using an angled
firing pin
Lowland Brigade Depot

A Martini action with the pivoted block in the
downward position ready for loading. The pivoting
block is controlled by the under lever. A striker is
contained in the block
Lowland Brigade Depot

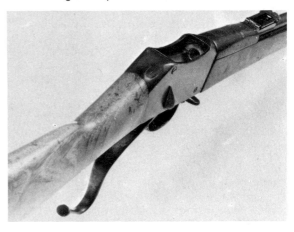

The breech block in the open
position. Notice how the
hammer in its downward
position wedges the block
closed, and the recoil is taken
on the lug on the underside of
the block
Lowland Brigade Depot

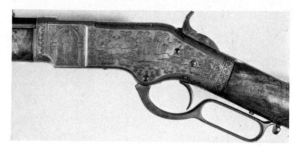

The lever action—this example is a Winchester '66
Pattern Room, Enfield

A forward hinged breech block shown in the open
position
Lowland Brigade Depot

The two vertical locking bolts slide up through the
sides of the receiver into the bolt itself and are
clearly visible on this Winchester 1892
J. B. Hall

The vertical blocks
having been withdrawn
allow the bolt to slide
rearward. Notice the
slots in the bolt for the
locking pieces
J. B. Hall

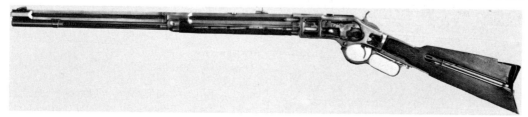

The 1873 Winchester sectioned to show the
tubular magazine under the barrel, the lever action
with its attendant linkages
Smithsonian Institution

A Mauser rifle Model 1835 manufactured by FN.
This is a simple bolt action rifle
Fabrique Nationale

The straight pull bolt which is operated as the name suggests by a pull directly to the rear is exemplified by the Swiss Schmidt-Ruben. For an illustration of the bolt in the closed position reference should be made to the Colour Illustrations
Lowland Brigade Depot

A rotating bolt in the closed position. Notice also the magazine cut-off to the right of the rifle body
Lowland Brigade Depot

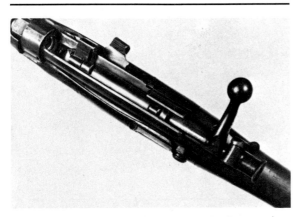

A rotating bolt shown partially retracted. With the rotating bolt action the bolt has to be lifted and then pulled to the rear. It is therefore theoretically marginally slower than the straight pull type. Also it is marginally easier to use when the weapon is at the shoulder
Lowland Brigade Depot

BLOWBACK WITH ADVANCED PRIMER IGNITION
The simplest form of improvement to the basic blowback system is to employ the inertia of the bolt on its forward movement to add to the effective weight of the bolt. The primer of the cartridge being chambered is fired when the bolt has still to contact the breech face. In the case of a typical weapon, the L2A3 submachine gun, the distance from breech face to chamber face is ·08in. The rearward force of the pressure therefore has not only to overcome the weight of the breech block but also its inertia as it is travelling in the opposite direction to the force. The force required to change the direction of the bolt and overcome the recoil spring is therefore considerable and reduces the weight required for the breech block. The blowback system can normally only be used with a low powered cartridge because of the danger of the cartridge being damaged on ejection and allowing an escape of high pressure gas, but with suitable delaying actions it can be used in weapons of 20mm or 30mm.

The pressure generated on firing a service rifle round is of the order of 50,000psi. The pressure is equally distributed about the case walls and base and thus the case walls are held against the chamber sides by this pressure. A straight blowback weapon would, because of the thrust rearward on the case head, allow the breech block to move to the rear. The result of the case head moving and the case walls not being able to is that the case ruptures. A partial solution to the problem is the use of this pressure to float the case clear of the chamber walls. A number of flutes are cut in the walls down which the gas can bleed. One method to enable the blowback type of action to be used with a high powered cartridge is to use a form of delay so that the pressure can drop to a reasonable level for case extraction.

Retard or Delayed Blowback
There are two forms of retarded blowback: mechanical and gas. The latter has been little used but two systems were used by the German development concerns during the closure of World War II.

GAS DELAY
The first system is used in the Volksturm Gewehr rifle. The operation of the bolt is controlled by continuing the bolt forward to surround the barrel. This acts as a piston and cylinder and when the rearward operation starts, gas is bled into this cylinder, thus forcing against the fore end of the bolt extension and slowing its movement.

The second system often named the Grossfus after the manufacturers utilises a block which is held against the bolt by gas pressure. The angle of the block and bolt is critical and the system has not been developed.

MECHANICAL DELAY
A mechanical delay can be brought about by a number of different systems. The first is the mechanical disadvantage in a link or toggle system by the use of carefully chosen angles and lengths. This mechanical delay system has been dropped in most weapons in favour of the lever or roller systems.

The pump action weapon is exemplified by this
Winchester Model '93 Shotgun
Winchester Gun Museum

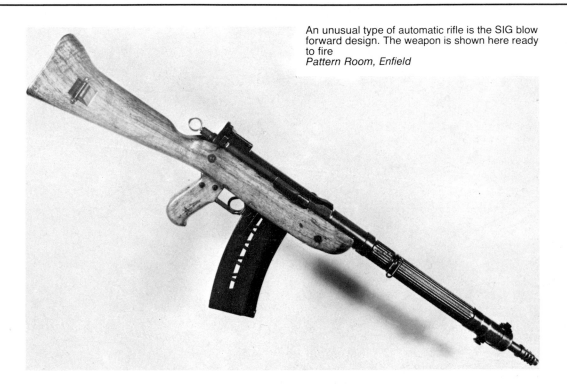

An unusual type of automatic rifle is the SIG blow
forward design. The weapon is shown here ready
to fire
Pattern Room, Enfield

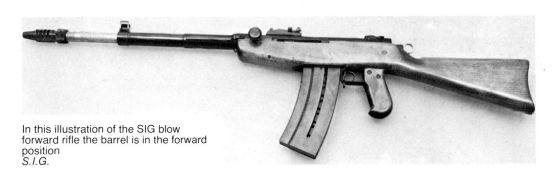

In this illustration of the SIG blow
forward rifle the barrel is in the forward
position
S.I.G.

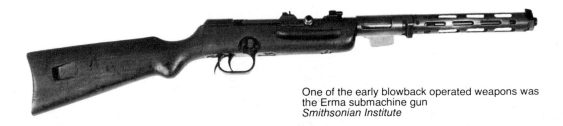

One of the early blowback operated weapons was
the Erma submachine gun
Smithsonian Institute

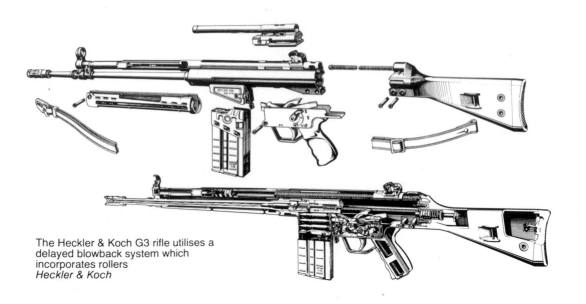

The Heckler & Koch G3 rifle utilises a
delayed blowback system which
incorporates rollers
Heckler & Koch

A blowback weapon is essentially of a simple construction. Here shown are the basic components—the
barrel, bolt, recoil spring and the main weapon body incorporating magazine and shoulder stock
C. Thompson

THE TOGGLE DELAYED BLOWBACK

A typical example of the link delay is that used on the Austrian Schwarzlose machine gun and consists of a bolt that is attached to the receiver by two links pivoted in the middle. This system although using a toggle is totally different from that on the Luger pistol. When the bolt is in the closed position the link is closed with the two arms almost parallel to the bolt centre line facing forward. The rearward force of firing tries to straighten the links and because of the angles involved this causes a delay sufficient to allow the pressure to drop to an acceptable level for extraction. The disadvantage of this system is that the links are somewhat bulky and thus it has been largely superseded by the roller system.

THE ROLLER DELAYED BLOWBACK

The roller and lever systems, such as that used on the H & K, and AA-52 GPMG all use a two-piece bolt. The two rollers which, when the bolt is forward, are held by the rear part of the bolt into the recesses in the receiver, lock the action. The rearward motion of the bolt must first force these rollers out of the recesses back into the bolt and thus allow it to move rearwards freely. This is delayed by the rear half of the bolt holding the rollers in place.

THE LEVER SYSTEM

The lever system used in the French GPMG AA-52 is similar to the roller system in that the lever is forced out of the breech block into engagement with the recess in the receiver by the second part of the block. The recoil energy has to force the rear part of the block via the lever backwards so that the lever clears the recess and the front and rear of the bolt can recoil.

Another type of lever is that used in the SIG weapon range; this uses a system which is in effect pivoted rollers. This works in the same manner as that described above.

BLISH SYSTEM

Another type of delayed blowback is the Blish 'H' lock which is used in the Thompson submachine gun. This system depends on the resistance to movement created by the friction caused by carefully angled surfaces. The 'H' piece rides in 70° rearward facing slots in the bolt and is free to move up and down in these slots. The receiver has two rearward facing slots machined in it at 45° and two projecting lugs on the 'H' piece can engage in them. The action works in the following sequence: the bolt in a forward position forces the 'H' piece downwards so that the 45° lugs are in engagement with slots in the receiver. The rearward force on the breech block on firing forces the bolt back trying to disengage the lugs, but the 'H' piece has to slide up the 70° slots for this to happen. As a result there is a delay while the friction of the faces is overcome. By the time this friction has been overcome the pressure has dropped to a safe level and the bolt opens. The problem with the system is that the

A typical example of blowback operation is the Rexim. In this illustration the bolt and recoil spring are clearly visible. Notice also the muzzle break with the slots designed to reduce the climb of the muzzle on automatic fire. A bayonet was also fitted standard to this weapon
Lowland Brigade Depot

An example of modern technique in construction is the blowback Franchi submachine gun
C. Thompson

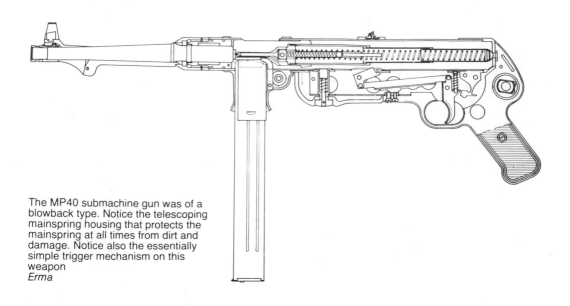

The MP40 submachine gun was of a blowback type. Notice the telescoping mainspring housing that protects the mainspring at all times from dirt and damage. Notice also the essentially simple trigger mechanism on this weapon
Erma

A weapon that also uses a rotating barrel lock is the French MAB. The cam is clearly shown on this illustration
G. Wilson

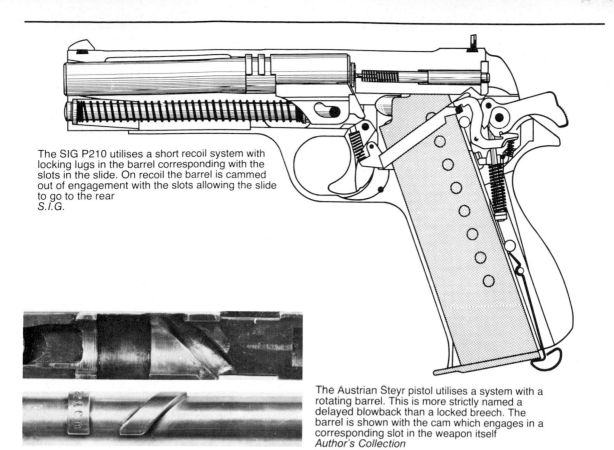

The SIG P210 utilises a short recoil system with locking lugs in the barrel corresponding with the slots in the slide. On recoil the barrel is cammed out of engagement with the slots allowing the slide to go to the rear
S.I.G.

The Austrian Steyr pistol utilises a system with a rotating barrel. This is more strictly named a delayed blowback than a locked breech. The barrel is shown with the cam which engages in a corresponding slot in the weapon itself
Author's Collection

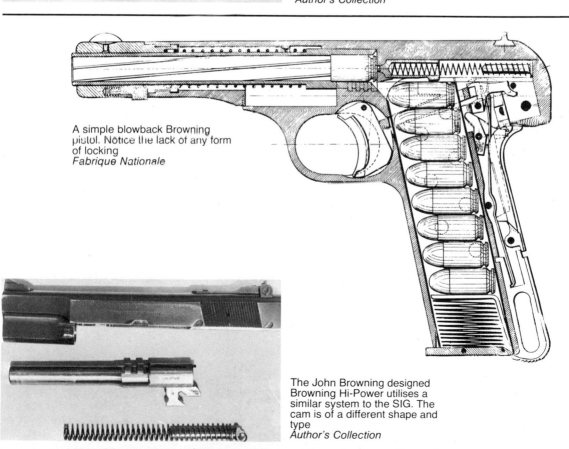

A simple blowback Browning pistol. Notice the lack of any form of locking
Fabrique Nationale

The John Browning designed Browning Hi-Power utilises a similar system to the SIG. The cam is of a different shape and type
Author's Collection

friction does not remain at a constant level even with the use of an oiler and thus the system has not been developed.

Gas and Recoil Actions
The actions described are all of the locked breech type and utilise many of the basic types of actions described previously.

Short Recoil
Short recoil features the breech remaining locked only long enough for the gas pressure to drop to a safe point.

Long Recoil
The long recoil system features the recoil of the barrel and barrel extension along with the breech block until the point for extraction is reached. The unlocking then takes place and the barrel group moves forward extracting the empty case. The breech block then returns forward and chambers a fresh round. Various types of locking systems are used with the long recoil weapons such as a rotating bolt head on the Frommer pistol and horizontally sliding breech on the Rarden cannon.

Toggle Lock
The toggle lock is usually identified with the Luger pistol. The principle used is similar to that of the knee joint on the human body. The toggle link remains straight and the breech closed as long as the pivots remain in a line. Once the toggle is forced out of line it buckles and the breech block can recoil. The breaking is usually brought about by the recoil of the breech block and barrel over cams. Both the Maxim and Vickers machine guns utilise this type of locking system.

Lug Lock
The two major types of lug lock are the Colt and Browning pistol type that utilise lugs on the barrel which engage in corresponding lugs in the gun's slide, thus holding them solidly together. On recoil the lugs are either pulled out of engagement by links on the Colt or cammed out in the Browning. The second type that finds much use in all types of weapon is the separate lug piece that locks the slide or breech block with the receiver. This locking lug is cammed out of engagement by the action of some moving parts e.g. a gas piston or cam, thus freeing the two components. The Walther P38 and the Nambu are examples of this type of lock on pistols.

Rotating Bolt
This system is infrequently used as a recoil action but has a great amount of inherent strength. The Germans however favoured it for use in their machine guns including the MG34. The basis is similar to the bolt action. The unlocking of the action is either accomplished by a cam, which as the recoil begins, turns a separate bolt head or, by the use of a rotating barrel such as the Steyre Model 1912 which is caused to rotate by the recoil energy.

The first of the John Browning locked breech designs featured a twin link system. The weapon shown is the earliest—the 1900 Series ·38 AC Automatics
J. Grieve

The later development by John Browning was the single link locking system. The weapon shown here is the Colt 1911
Author's Collection

A SIG P210. This cutaway weapon shows clearly the locking lugs on the barrel and slide
S.I.G.

The vertical sliding breech block shown on the Wombat Anti Tank Gun is in the closed position

The Wombat breech slid vertically downwards to the open position ready for loading

The toggle action of the Luger is clearly shown. This is a short recoil weapon utilising the movement of the barrel to the rear to push the toggle out of alignment thereby opening the breech
Pierre Claude Tilley—Blitz Publications

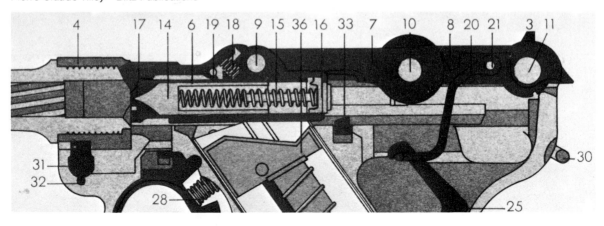

One of the oddest forms of machine gun is the Madsen. The weapon utilises the Martini type of action controlled by a side plate
Lowland Brigade Depot

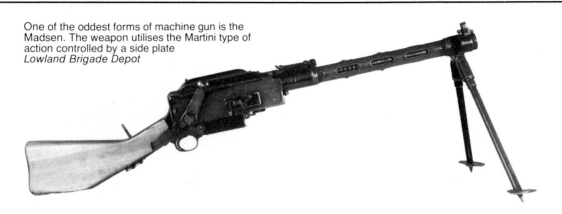

Gas Action

The gas operated systems are divided into three separate types: short stroke piston, long stroke piston and direct gas action.

SHORT STROKE PISTON

Short stroke piston utilises gas tapped from the barrel to give it motion. The piston has no direct connection with the bolt or the operating rod but gives a short sharp blow to initiate the unlocking cycle. The Piston does not follow but is returned directly to its position by a return spring. The type of locking arrangement used with the weapon varies but all are operated by the action of the piston.

LONG STROKE PISTON

The long stroke piston travels full distance coupled by a piston extension of the breech block. The piston extension operates the unlocking of the breech which can be of any type.

The long stroke piston is the most commonly used for automatic weapons such as the LMG and MMG but the short stroke piston has the advantage of less operating weight and thus is used for the rifle.

DIRECT GAS ACTION

The direct gas action feeds the gas back to operate directly on the breech locking system. The pressure of the gas itself is the means of unlocking as opposed to the piston or the piston extension of the two methods above. The problems with the direct gas action are the build up of carbon deposits in the operating parts leading to weapon malfunction if not cleaned at frequent intervals.

The Colt AR15 is a particularly large production example.

Tilting Breech Block

The tilting breech block is confined to the gas operated type of weapon. When the weapon is ready to fire the breech block is locked into the receiver. When fired the block is tilted out of engagement with the locking release and allowed to move rearwards.

Rotating Bolt

The rotating bolt system has become the most popular form of locking device in small arms. The AR18 manufactured by Sterling has a short stroke piston that delivers a thrust to a bolt carrier that holds a multi lug bolt which locks into a barrel extension. This energy causes the carrier to move rearwards and as it moves the bolt head is rotated out of engagement with the barrel extension by a cam running in a cam slot machined in the bolt carrier. The bolt then moves rearwards for the reloading cycle. The M.16 operates in a similar fashion but the initial impulse is imparted by direct gas action.

Primer Projection

The primer projection method of operation depends on the setting back of the primer on firing. This can only be used with a special round with a primer that is designed to move back on firing. The rearward motion of the primer is used to unlock the breech mechanism. This method suffers from the disadvantage of needing a special type of ammunition for reliable operation.

The long recoil system is little used for infantry weapons, however the French Chauchaut Light Machine Gun used it. Notice the extremely long body necessary to accommodate the recoiling components
Lowland Brigade Depot

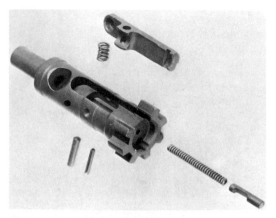

The modern type of rotating bolt is shown with its multi locking lugs and extractor in this ullustration of an AR18 bolt
Armalite Inc.

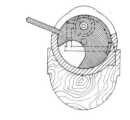

A cutaway of a rotating breech block. The left illustration shows the weapon in the ready to fire position and the right in the loading position
Andrew Yule

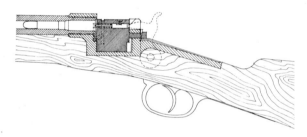

A rotating breech block in the firing position
Andrew Yule

A rotating breech block rotated so that the empty case may be removed
Andrew Yule

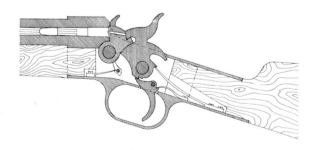

The Remington rolling block action. Notice that the breech block has been rotated rearwards to allow the weapon to be loaded
Andrew Yule

A Remington rolling block in the fired position. Notice the hammer has a cam on the bottom part which engages with the breech block thus locking the action
Andrew Yule

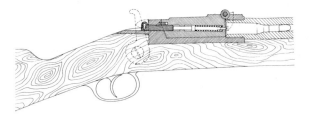

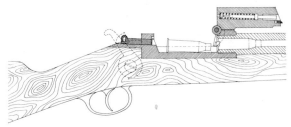

A Springfield forward hinged breech block. This
gave it a name the Trapdoor Springfield
Andrew Yule

Springfield Trapdoor in the ready to load or reject
position
Andrew Yule

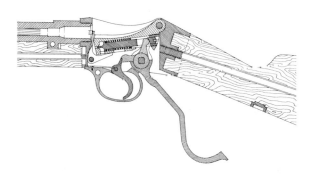

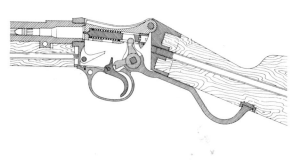

The Martini action ready to load. Notice that the
striker is combined in the block
Andrew Yule

The Martini action in the fired position
Andrew Yule

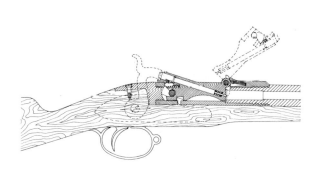

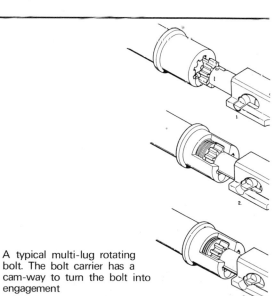

A further form of forward hinged breech block
compared to that of the Springfield
Andrew Yule

A typical multi-lug rotating
bolt. The bolt carrier has a
cam-way to turn the bolt into
engagement

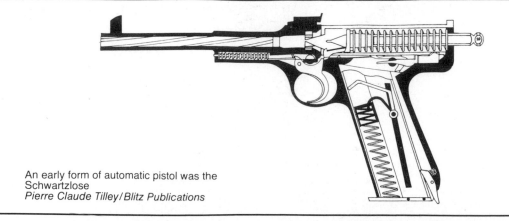

An early form of automatic pistol was the
Schwartzlose
Pierre Claude Tilley/Blitz Publications

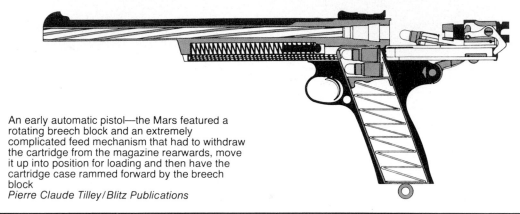

An early automatic pistol—the Mars featured a
rotating breech block and an extremely
complicated feed mechanism that had to withdraw
the cartridge from the magazine rearwards, move
it up into position for loading and then have the
cartridge case rammed forward by the breech
block
Pierre Claude Tilley/Blitz Publications

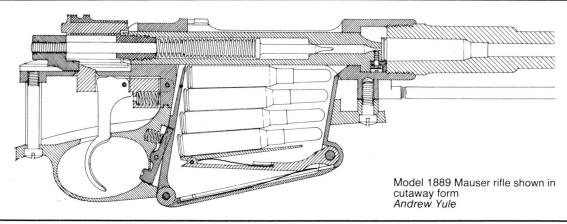

Model 1889 Mauser rifle shown in
cutaway form
Andrew Yule

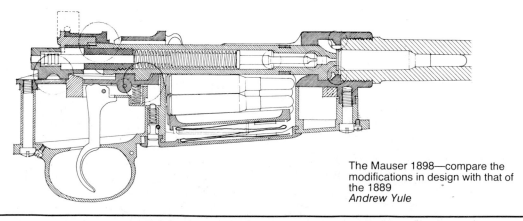

The Mauser 1898—compare the
modifications in design with that of
the 1889
Andrew Yule

A PIAT or Projector Infantry Anti Tank which was a spigot mortar. It is shown here being loaded
Imperial War Museum

Chapter 6

Anti-Tank Weapons, Grenades and Mortars

The first confrontation between armour and the infantryman came with the adoption of comprehensive body armour by the knight. The first anti-armour weapon was the bow and arrow and particularly the crossbow bolt. The arrival of the gun made the body armour obsolete; the infantryman had won the first round.

Anti-tank weapons by the very nature of the requirement to penetrate better and better armour have developed out of all recognition. The thickness of the armour has increased from 8–12mm of the First World War using in many cases a near vertical plate to 150mm sloped front plate on the Second World War Tiger II. The sloping of the armour has two important effects, the actual thickness increases with the increase in slope and the effect of the armour piercing ammunition is degraded.

Armour of 100mm is, in practice, 200mm thick if it is inclined at an angle of 60° and has an effective thickness compared with a vertical plate of some 300mm. To add to the problems of the anti-tank weapon a spaced-off plate has been used in some cases to detonate charges away from the main armour.

The first attempt to provide the infantryman with some means of penetrating the armour was the logical one of manufacturing a larger rifle, and in February 1918 the German army was equipped with a 13mm Mauser anti-tank rifle. This weapon was merely a scaled-up Mauser bolt action rifle and was capable of penetrating 20mm of armour at 90° but it weighed over 17kg and has a very high recoil.

The end of the war saw the banning of these weapons for Germany by the Allies, who themselves rushed in the inter-war years to perfect anti-tank rifles of their own. The various attempts all resulted in weapons which were very heavy and had heavy recoils. The British in 1938 developed the Boys anti-tank rifle which, with a bore of ·55in and using a steel cored bullet, was inferior to the First World War Mauser rifle. The Russians introduced two rifles, the Degtyarev and the Simonov in 1944. These weapons used ammunition with a tungsten core and could penetrate 30mm of armour. The anti tank rifle proved inefficient against the German armour and the idea of a rifle-based weapon with its weight and heavy recoil disappeared.

Armour had won the second round.

The shaped charge was to be the single most important development in the development of the anti-tank weapon as it could penetrate great thicknesses of armour. The shaped charge was discovered by an American C. E. Munro in the last century and the effect is therefore sometimes known by that name. The effect is obtained by the use of a cone shaped liner that acts as a focusing device for the explosive force. The explosive is detonated from the rear and the resultant stream of molten metal and gas act as a cutting torch and burn their way through the armour. The two points brought out by the experiments done by various combatants were that the effect of the charge was degraded if there was any rotation and that the effect was increased very conciderably by the increase in diameter of the cone.

A German anti tank rifle shown converted to fire anti tank grenades. This was done owing to its inability in standard form to penetrate armour
Imperial War Museum

In 1941 the Germans utilised the hollow charge principle in a fin-stabilised rifle launched grenade. The British also used the 68 grenade with a similar principle. These anti-tank grenades were, however, only marginally more efficient than the earlier weapons. The other type of anti-armour grenade issued to the infantry was the 'Sticky Bomb' which as the name indicates was designed to stick to the outside of the tank and thus hold the explosive in the best place to do damage. This had at least two disadvantages, the thrower had to be rather too close and the grenade could stick to him! The simpler Molotov cocktail is much more easily manufactured and probably more effective. This consists of a container with an inflammable liquid, usually a bottle filled with petrol, which when it bursts is ignited by some means such as a burning rag. This has the effect of boiling the occupants of

the tank if not destroying the vehicle itself.

The British in 1942 developed the Platoon Infantry Anti-Tank Weapon or PIAT. This used a spigot launched hollow charged bomb and worked in the following manner. The weapon was cocked (a most unpopular process as the effort required against the spring was considerable), the bomb was placed in the discharger ramp, the weapon aimed and the trigger pulled. The spigot propelled by the spring was driven forward and ignited the propellant charge that drove the bomb out of the trough towards the target. Back pressure of the gas cocked the weapon's spring ready for another bomb. The range was limited to under 100yd and the thickness of armour pierced depended on the bomb hitting at the near vertical when it could penetrate as much as 8–10in.

The Germans' first attempt to utilise the shaped charge other than in the form of a grenade was the

A Carl Gustaf anti tank gun. The breech is open and the round is being loaded
Crown Copyright

Panzerfaust which was in effect a recoilless gun. It operated by the burning of the propellant in a small diameter tube which was the means of holding the weapon, the projectile of larger diameter went forward and the gases backwards and thus the two balanced and gave a recoilless action.

The American forces were the first to be equipped with the rocket launcher type of weapon, often called the Bazooka. This was simply a tube from which a shaped charge warhead rocket was fired. The rocket was fin-stabilised and thus the charge was not degraded by rotation. The one problem with this and the other rocket-firing weapons developed by the Germans and the British was, and is, that the rocket exhaust which is emitted from the rear of the tube is dangerous to other troops and needless to say gives away the position of the firer.

The Americans continued to develop the recoilless gun and before the end of the war were using it in combat. The recoilless rifle used by the Americans worked on the same principle as the German Panzerfaust in that the recoil was balanced by the rearward flow of the gases. The Americans, however, fired the round from a tube similar to that of the Bazooka. The tube has therefore to be able to withstand the pressure of the gases that can be in the region of two and a half times that in the rocket launcher. The advantage is an increase in the muzzle velocity over that of the rocket of some three times, although as much as four-fifths of the gases of the propellant are diverted to the rear. The range is, needless to say, nothing like that of a standard weapon firing the same size of shell. The barrels are often rifled and thus a variety of methods are used to stop the explosive charge from rotating. One method uses a driving band that rotates round the charge and a second consists of mounting the charge on two rollers or ball bearings and thus the outer casing only rotates. Both of these do not stop rotation but help to keep it within acceptable limits. Weapons that do not use a rifled barrel utilise fins that spring out as the shell leaves the barrel and thus drag-stabilise the shell. A typical weapon of this type is the Karl Gustaf which operates as follows: the charge with a rupture disc at its rear is attached by its casing to the shell. The propellant is ignited and the resulting pressure breaks the spigot joining the shell to the case and at the same time the rupture disc breaks so that as the shell leaves the barrel the recoil force is balanced by the gases exhausted from the rear of the launcher. The same problem as with the rocket is therefore present from the backblast.

The final development in the anti-tank weapon was to provide a form of guidance for the projectile when it has left the projector. The first generation guided anti-tank missiles utilise a rocket that is wire-guided and is visually tracked by the firer by a flare at the rear. The firer can, by means of a control, alter the fins on the missile and thus alter the direction of travel. The second generation utilise the wire system, but, with the control movements being automatic, the firer only needs to keep the target in the sights of the command unit and the course corrections are made by the control unit. Both of these weapons use HEAT warheads in the main. Although not directly connected to small arms, the following definition of initials is in common use in the anti-tank vocabulary.

APC—this is the oldest type of armour piercing shell. The Armour Piercing Capped Projectile has an armour piercing core covered with a ballistic cap. The ballistic cap ensures the same impact point as standard ammunition while allowing the ideal shape of core.

APDS—the method used to increase the velocity of an armour piercing round is to use a discarding sabot that enables the use of a small diameter core which can be fired in the larger bore by the use of the sabot. The Armour Piercing Discarding Sabot is a round in current use. A disadvantage is that the sabot can do damage when discarded.

A second generation anti tank weapon—a Milan. Notice the soldier on the right with the aiming unit, the infantryman on the left has a spare round
Aerospatiale

HESH—the High Explosve Squash Head utilises the principle of not penetrating the armour in all cases but places a relatively large amount of explosive in the shape of a cow pat on the surface of the armour. The result is that the metal on the reverse side scabs off into the interior of the tank and thus kills the occupants. The charge will also do considerable damage to the exterior.

The Grenade

The grenade is older than gunpowder. In fact the principle of throwing rocks, molten lead or later Greek fire dates from the beginning of warfare itself. The principle of Greek fire was utilised in the incendiary grenade and the hand thrown round cannon-ball-like bomb with the cannon fuse preceded the modern high explosive hand grenade. The grenade has developed little from those early attempts as the basic principle has never been modified and the only change has been in the increase in efficiency by the use of modern materials. The basic types of grenade used in the Second World War may be taken as typical examples of the present day ones as they only vary in the type or power of the explosives. One point that the reader must bear in mind is that, if a grenade or for that matter any explosive device, should ever come into his or her possession it must never be considered safe as the age may have made the explosives unstable. Never believe the previous owner's assurance that it is harmless or has no explosive filling. The basic types of grenade, high explosive and smoke/incendiary are split as follows: pure anti-personnel, high explosive with anti-personnel effect, high explosive demolition, anti-tank, smoke or incendiary and rifle grenades of all previous types.

The anti-personnel grenade utilises an explosive charge to produce lethal metal shrapnel from a fragmentable liner or cover. Typical examples are the British 36 grenade and Mills bomb, the German stick grenade fitted with the fragmentable cover, the American Mark II and the Russian F1. These grenades all utilise a delay fuse which allows the thrower to be clear of the direct blast. The present British and American grenade for anti-personnel use is the US M26/L2A1 and utilises an RDX/TNT explosive core with a tin plate case. The fragmentable liner is made up of wire that is notched at ⅛in intervals and thus breaks up into over 1000 particles that have an effective range of five metres. A modern trend is to make the grenade smaller using the advances in explosives to produce the same effect. A mini-grenade from the firm of NWM weighs only five ounces but with its fragmentable case can inflict damage to persons within a five metre radius and it can be thrown up to 70yd.

The high explosive grenade uses the force of a relatively large amount of explosive to give either blast effect against personnel or a limited amount of structural damage to buildings or vehicles.

The blast effect also has a considerable anti-morale effect even if the person is not within lethal range. Examples of this type are the British 69, the American Mark III, the German Egg grenade or the Stick grenade without the fragmentable cover.

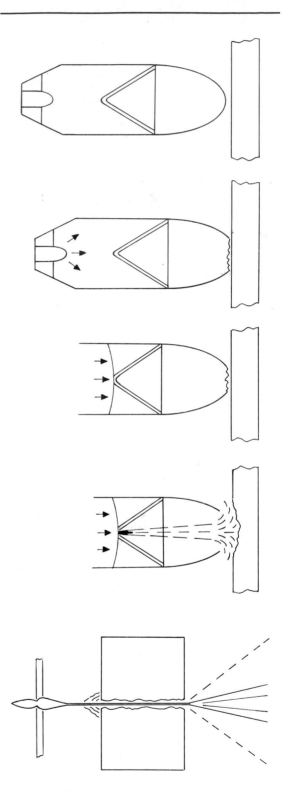

A diagram showing the effect of a hollow-charge warhead on armour plate. Notice the charge is detonated from the rear and that the hollow cone is held off from the plate by the nosecone of the missile. The high velocity gas jet containing particles of metal from the cone acts as a cutting torch and burns its way through the plate

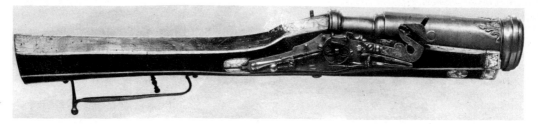

An early attempt at a grenade launcher—A wheellock weapon
Glasgow Art Gallery and Museum

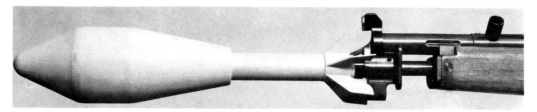

A rifle grenade in position ready for firing. This system enabled the infantryman to project either smoke or anti tank grenades to a considerable distance

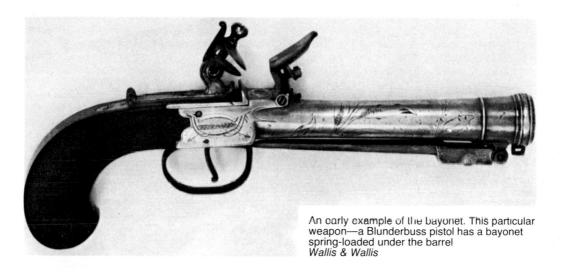

An early example of the bayonet. This particular weapon—a Blunderbuss pistol has a bayonet spring-loaded under the barrel
Wallis & Wallis

A simple German anti-tank weapon from WWII is the Panzerfaust. This was easily portable and was a one-shot throw away weapon

The anti-tank grenade has already been mentioned under anti-tank weapons. Typical types used were hand thrown or placed; British 73 thermos flask, 74 sticky bomb, Nawkins 75 grenade mine. By and large the anti-tank grenade was a failure as the user had to be rather closer than was safe to use it efficiently and even then the effect was limited. The Japanese used a variant that needed supreme courage as it was a grenade attached to a sort of broomstick with which it was held against the hull of The phosphorus type of grenade gives out intense heat but, more important for general use, it creates a dense cloud of smoke. This allows a foot soldier to carry his own smoke-screen so that he may extricate himself from difficulties.

In an attempt to provide a greater than throwing range and utlise the infantryman's own weapons the rifle grenade came into being. The first use of the rifle grenade was probably as early as 1660 when a stick type was used by the Swedish Infantry. The stick grenade used the standard musket or rifle to launch a small grenade that is attached to a stick. The stick is loaded down the barrel and the fuse of the grenade arranged to start on firing and explode at the target. The danger of the first weapons of this type was that with the fuse on the grenade being hand lit the weapon could, with the methods of ignition available, misfire. This left the poor fellow with a grenade attached to the end of the weapon and about to explode! The development of the stick grenade was limited to the use of a more efficient fuse and they were used in the the First World War by both sides in quantity, and also in the Second World War with such weapons as the Russian anti-tank stick grenade.

The second of the types of musket—or rifle-launched grenades used the discharger cup. The discharger cup was in use as early as 1700 using a cup mounted on the end of a musket and a blank charge with a large wad at the base of the cup to seal the gas. The discharger cup has changed little, even the Second World War 36 British anti-personnel grenade and the 68 anti-tank grenade using the same principle.

The modern type of rifle grenade uses no grenade cup but is projected from the end of the barrel either with an extension or on some weapons an integral launcher. A typical example is the Frim which has a thin casing and an HE lining with steel balls embedded in it. The problem with rifle grenades is the very much increased recoil, especially true of the modern lightweight assault rifles. This can be as much as 700%, leading to damage of the weapon—thus the grenade launcher is coming more into favour.

The final use of the grenade is in the specifically designed grenade launcher which is a near relation of the mortar. The use of the weapons was started in the seventeenth century. The early weapons were muzzle loading and projected small bore grenades over short distances. This type of weapon went unaltered until the development of the breech loader and the the cartridge. A typical example of the early development is the Walther Kampfpistole which fired small explosive anti-tank or anti-personnel grenades. The latest type of launcher, the M79, fires a number of different projectiles including a bouncing bomb which by means of an auxiliary explosive charge blows itself back into the air on initial impact so as to give a better spread of the fragments.

The development of the mortar ranged from the hand-held grenade launchers described previously to the simple muzzle loading ones developed at the same time as the first cannon. The mortar is a weapon that fires a projectile over a relatively short range with a high trajectory. The early mortars or bombards continued little altered up to the twentieth century when the mortar, although still muzzle loaded, used a combined propellant charge and projectile. The fin-stabilised projectile was either fired by the action of a fixed firing pin in the base of the mortar tube or by means of a lanyard and a separate firing pin mechanism. The mortar therefore is unique in that it has basically never been anything but a muzzle loader. Modern mortars fire both HE and smoke/incendiary—for example the typical light mortar used during the Second World War, the

A very typical example of the infantryman's mortar in action. This is the British 2″ mortar in use during the Second World War
Imperial War Museum

British 2in. This weapon is basically a tube fitted by means of a pivoted mounting to a base plate or spade. The range was from 100–500 yards and HE, smoke illuminating or signal could be fired. The German equivalent was the SCM GRW36, and the Japanese the so-called 'knee' mortar. The present British light mortar is the 81mm.

One modern development is the mortar projectile with rocket assistance; a second development which is a deterrent to the use of the mortar is the anti-mortar radar which can plot back the trajectory of the bomb and allow counter measures.

Other specialist weapons used extensively by the Infantry were the flame thrower and the Bangalore wire destroyer. The flame thrower is not a new weapon as the exponents of the Greek fire in the pre-gunpowder days had already realised the effectiveness of the flame as an offensive and defensive weapon. The weapon did not see wide use until the Second World War when the need to ferret out defenders in foxholes and concrete emplacements became very necessary. The first flame throwers were not very reliable but the later weapons had a range of about fifty yards and gave ten two-second blasts of flame. The fuel was carried in one container and the gas to project it out in another. The trigger mechanism worked an igniter, usually a form of blank cartridge and gas was released to force the liquid out of the nozzle.

The Bangalore torpedo is used to clear barbed wire and other entanglements by means of a widely placed explosive charge. The charge is contained within long tubes which can be joined together to make any length necessary.

These weapons with the addition of the bayonet make up the infantryman's personal offensive and defensive armament.

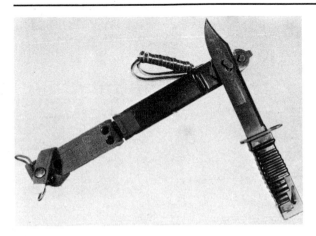

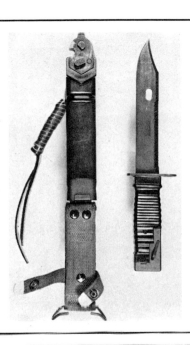

An example of the latest trend in bayonet which combines not only a bayonet for attachment to the rifle but also a fighting knife, a saw and an insulated pair of wire cutters
Pattern Room, Enfield

A fighting knife come bayonet shown fitted to an Armalite AR18
Armalite Inc.

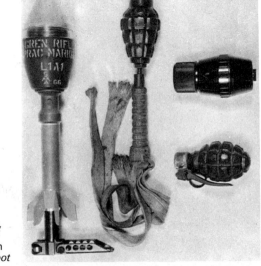

A variety of grenade, either rifle launched (left) or hand thrown
Lowland Brigade Depot

This list contains some of the more famous names associated with firearms.

Name	Description	Date
Adams, Robert	Double action revolver	1851
Allen, Ethan	Pepperbox 1837	1806–1871
Allin, E. S.	Conversions muzzle to breech loader 1865	1809–1879
Armstrong	Inventor and developer of firearms	
Bacon, F.	First recorder of the constituents of gunpowder	1260
Baker, Ezekiel	Muzzle loading weapons	1800–1838
Ballard, C. H.	Breech loaders 1861	
Berdan, Col Hiram	Inventor of the primer	1869–1892
Beretta, Claudio	Founder of the firm	1580–1640
Bergmann, T.	Inventor of automatic pistols and other firearms	1894–1903
Billinghurst, W.	Battery gun inventor	1807–1880
Borchardt, Hugo	Rifle and pistol designer	1876–1893
Boss, Thomas	Shotguns	1832–1859
Boxer, E. M.	Inventor of the primer	
Browning, J. M.	The greatest firearms inventor and gun maker	1855–1926
Brunswick	Inventor of a rifle and rifling	
Burgess, A.	Magazine and automatic weapons	1837–1908
Burnside, A. E.	Breech loader	1824–1881
Campogiro, Count	Inventor of an automatic pistol	1920
Carcano	Italian bolt action	1868
Chassepot, A.	French rifle inventor	1833–1905
Collier, E. H.	Flintlock revolver	1817–1850
Colt, Samuel	Designer and inventor	1814–1862
Dean	Inventor of revolvers	
Delvigne, A.	Breech designer	1799–1876
Degtyarev, Vasily	Russian automatic weapon designer	Current
Derringer, H.	Gunmaker, Name given to the type of pistol	1806–1869
Dreyse, J. N.	Inventor of the needle gun	1787–1867
Egg, Durs	Gunmaker	1777–1834
Egg, Joseph	Gunmaker	1785–1815
Federov, D. G.	Russian designer	1924
Flobert, L.	Inventor of the rimfire	1864
Forsyth, A. J.	Percussion lock inventor	1768–1843
Fosbery	Inventor of the automatic revolver	
Garand, J. C.	Developer of the Garand rifle	1887
Gatling, R. J.	Inventor of the Gatling gun	1818–1903
Gras	Inventor	1874
Greener, W. W.	Gunmaker	1827–1869
Hall, J. H.	Inventor and gunmaker	1811–1840
Henry, B. T.	Inventor and developer	1821–1898
Hotchkiss, B. B.	Inventor	1826–1885
Hunt, Walter	Inventor	1859
Jacob, J.	Rifling	1858
Janson, F.	EM2 British designer now with Winchester	Current
Jennings, Lewis	Inventor tube magazine breech loader	1849–1851
Jessen, N. S.	Inventor pillar breech and oval bore	1829–1862
Kalthoff, Mathias	Repeating weapon	1646–1672
Kalthoff, Peter	Repeating breech loading weapons	1641–1672
Kalashicov	Russian designer of firearms	
Klett, (Family)	Gunmakers	1550–1750
Krag, Ole H.	Bolt action magazine rifle	1837–1912
Kropatschek, Alfred von	Tubular magazine bolt action rifle	1870–1885
Krupp, Alfred	Cannon manufacturer	1810–1887
Lancaster, Charles	Inventor, oval bore rifling	1848–1855
Lebel, Nicolas	Tubular magazine bolt action rifle	1835–1891
Lee, James	Straight pull magazine rifle	1831–1904
Lefaucheux, Eugene	Pinfire inventor	1820–1871
Le Mat, Dr Alex	Revolver designer	1855–1865
Lorenzoni	Repeating flintlock	
Luger, Georg	Developer of Borchardt into Luger pistol	1889–1907
Lyman, William	Founder Lyman Gunsight Co	1878–1898
Mannlicher, Ferdinand Ritter von	Clip feed inventor	1848–1904
Marengoni, Tullio	Italian designer, worked for Beretta	
Manton, John and Joseph	Gunmakers	1766–1835
Marlin, John M.	Revolver and rifle manufacturer	1870–1915
Martini, Friedrich	Inventor (Martini-Henry) rifle	1869
Mauser, Paul	Gun designer	1838–1914
Maxim, Sir Hiram S.	Inventor machine gun	1840–1916
Maynard, Dr Edward	Gun inventor—tape primer	1845–1886
Metford	Inventor and developer of rifling type	
Minié, Claude E.	Inventor of Minié rifle and bullet	1814–1879
Mondragon, Manuel	Gas operated rifle inventor	1896–1907
Nambu, Colonel	Japanese designer	1930
Nagant, L.	Revolver and rifle designer	1875–1896
Nock, Henry	Gunmaker	1741–1804
Pauly, Samuel J.	Inventor of cartridges	1808–1821
Peabody, Henry	Rifle inventor	1862–1880
Pederson	Gun designer, invented rifles and Pederson device	1920
Prelat, Francois	French inventor	1810–1820
Puckle, James	Inventor revolving cannon	1720
Purdy, James	London gunmaker	1825–1879
Remington, E.	Arms manufacturer	1828
Requa, J.	Inventor Requa-Billinghurst battery gun	1860
Revelli	Italian gun designer (the Villar Perosa)	1915
Ross	Designer of the Ross rifle	
Root, E. K.	Designer revolver produced by Colt	1853–1857
Ruger, William	Gun manufacturer	Current
Salza, D.	Italian gun designer (Beretta)	Current
Sauer, J. P.	Gunmaker	1790–1820
Savage, Arthur W.	Gunmaker	1857–1938
Schofield, George W.	Inventor weapons produced by Smith & Wesson	1870–1880
Sharps, Christian	Gun designer and builder	1811–1874
Shaw, Joshua	Percussion cap patentee	1777–1860
Snider, Jacob	Breech conversion for British army	1859
Spencer, Christopher	Tube Magazine	1841–1920
Stoner, Gene	Military gun designer	Current
Thouvenin, Col Louis	Inventor of Tige or pillar breech	1843
Thuer, F.	Revolver patentee	1868–1870
Tokarev, F. V.	Russian designer	1871–1912
Tranter, William	Double action revolver	1846–1863
Vettereli, Frederich	Magazine rifle developer	1822–1882
Volcanic Repeating Arms Co	Repeating pistols and rifles	1855–1857
Walther, Karl	Weapons producer (pistols)	1917–1945
Webley, James	Gunmaker	1857–1864
Wesson, Daniel B.	Founded Smith & Wesson	1825–1906
Whitworth	Engineer—rifling developer	1850
Winchester, Oliver F.	Manufacturer and gunmaker	1810–1880

Accelerator	A device to help the action of some automatic weapons or to increase the rate of fire.
Accles Feed	A feed system for ammunition that uses the Accles principle.
ACP	Automatic Colt Pistol. Abbreviation is usually applied to the ammunition.
Action	The part of the weapon that contains the operational parts.
Air gun	A weapon that relies on air either compressed by hand or from a cylinder to propel the bullet.
Ammunition	The basic constituents of the means to discharge the weapon. Consists of the propellant, projectile and usually the method of ignition.
Anvil	The block that the priming compound is struck against by the firing pin. Can either be part of the primer or of the case.
AP	Armour piercing. There are many derivatives:
APC	Armour piercing capped.
APDS	Armour piercing discarding sabot.
Aperture sight	The type of sight that uses a small hole aperture as the rear element.
Armoury	The place of storage of weapons and their attendant military supplies.
Arquebus	A light portable weapon of the shoulder arm type. Not now used.
Arsenal	The place of manufacture of military supplies.
Artillery	Weapons such as wheeled guns of the larger type.
Autoloading	A weapon that carries out the operations of the weapon automatically but only once for each pull of the trigger.
Automatic	A weapon that performs the actions of loading, firing and ejecting with a pull of the trigger. True automatics continue to fire until the trigger is released. The modern use of the word such as in automatic pistol is not strictly correct but is common usage.
Backstrap	Part of the frame of a revolver or automatic pistol that forms the rear of the grip.
Ball (ammunition)	The standard round with a single projectile used for anti-personnel duty.
Ballistics	The science of the measurement of the performance of the propellant, primer and projectile.
Exterior ballistics	The science applied to the bullet in flight.
Interior ballistics	The science applied to the primer bullet and powder when the bullet is in the barrel.
Terminal ballistics	The science applied to the effect of the bullet on striking its target.
Band (barrel)	A band used to attach the barrel to the fore-end.
BAR	Browning Automatic Rifle.
Barleycorn (sight)	The use of a front sight in the shape of a grain of corn or an inverted 'V'.
Barrel	A tube used to guide the projectile.
Barrel band	A band used to attach the barrel to the fore-end of the weapon.
Barrel jacket	A protective cover for the barrel.
Battery cup	A type of primer that uses a separate cup containing the anvil. Used estensively in shot gun shells.
Bazooka	A nickname for the American rocket launcher used as an anti-tank weapon. Popularly used for all rocket launchers.
BB	Bulleted breech.
Bipod	A support for a weapon, usually a LMG or a GPMG, which has two legs.
Belt (cartridge)	A method of holding a number of cartridges ready to be fed into the weapon.
Belt (feed)	A type of feed utilising the cartridges held in a belt. (Two main types are solid that is continuous from end to end, and disintegrating which breaks up as it is fired.)
Bent	Part of the trigger mechanism.
Black powder	The first form of propellant so named from the vast amount of dense black smoke caused by the incomplete burning on firing.
Blank	A round of ammunition that has no projectile but produces noise and a flash.
Blowback	The type of weapon that uses the force of the gases on firing to blow back the breech. Also used to describe the escape of gases from the chamber if a cartridge case should rupture or a primer blow out.
Blueing	A rusting process or heat colouring used as a decorative and protective finish on firearms.
Blunderbuss	A weapon that has a barrel that increases in diameter greatly at the muzzle.
Bolt	The device used to close the rear end of the breech; usually contains elements of the locking arrangement. Takes its name from its similarity to the standard door bolt.

Bolt action	The type of weapon that uses the bolt system.
Bore	The internal surface of the barrel.
Bottleneck (as applied to a cartridge)	The type of case where the neck is smaller than the base with the difference caused by the use of a bottle-neck shaped constriction.
Box lock	A weapon where the lock mechanism is contained in a box-like container attached to the stock.
Box magazine	A magazine that is in the shape of a box.
Boxer primer	A primer invented by Colonel Boxer. It contains its own anvil and uses one central flash hole.
Breech	The rear end of the barrel where the weapon is loaded.
Breech-loader	The type of weapon which has a breech as opposed to the muzzle loader.
Browning	See Blueing.
Buffer	A device used in the action of some weapons to absorb some of the forces of recoil.
Bullet	The projectile usually of small calibre that is fired from a weapon.
Bulleted blank	As most automatic weapons of the recoil or gas operated system cannot obtain the necessary energy from a standard blank to operate the action, a blank with a bullet usually wood or plastic is used. The bullet is either destroyed at the muzzle or is a short range type for safety reasons.
Bull pup	A type of weapon having the action and feed system behind the pistol grip.
Bushing (barrel)	The part of the weapon which acts as a guide for the barrel during recoil.
Butt	The part of the weapon that is attached to the barrel to act as a rest for the shoulder, or a means of holding a pistol.
Butt plate	A plate attached to the base of the butt to protect it against damage.
Calibre	The size of the bore of a weapon. Can be measured in either metric or linear units, or as a gauge.
Cannon	A weapon that has as its means of firing a touch hole. Cannon ignition is the application of this type of ignition.
Cannon ignition	As above.
Cannelure	This is a groove either in a bullet or a case. In the bullet it can contain a lubricant or to hold the bullet in place in the case. On a case it is used to hold a bullet in place.
Cap	Term used to either denote a primer or the earlier percussion cap.
Carbine	A short version of a longarm.
Cartridge	A combination of a bullet and a propellant and usually a primer. Can be paper skin or in modern types a brass or steel container.
Case	The container for the primer and propellant in a cartridge
Centre fire	A cartridge or a weapon for a cartridge that has the primer in the centre. (See Rimfire.)
Chamber	The rear of the barrel or a separate container that houses the cartridge.
Charge	The amount or bulk of the propellant.
Charger	See Clip.
Choke	The reduction in the dimension of the bore of a shot firing weapon to give a controlled pattern of the shot.
Chronograph	An instrument for measuring the velocity of a bullet.
Clip	A holder for a number of cartridges to facilitate loading.
Cock	The early type of hammer on flintlock weapons.
Combustible cartridge	A cartridge case that is made from a combustible material and thus leaves no residue in the breech.
Compensator	A type of muzzle brake. This utilises the gases from the propellant to act as a counter to the recoil by diverting the gases upward and thus providing a downward force.
Concealed hammer	A hammer that is contained within the outer cover of the weapon.
Cordite	A propellant used for large bore cartridges.
Core	The centre of a bullet usually of some heavy metal such as lead. This is covered by a jacket of a harder metal, or in the case of an armour-piercing core a softer cover.
Corrosion	Corrosion in firearms is usually caused by either a corrosive primer or the use of black powder.
Creep	As applied to a trigger is the play in the linkage before the weapon fires.
Crimp	A crimp as applied to a cartridge is the forcing in of the case to grip the bullet.
Cut off	On the early magazine rifles the general staff thought the soldier was better to fire the weapon as a single shot, except in emergencies and so a magazine cut off to hold the cartridges in the magazine was devised.

Crane	The part of the revolver mechanism that allows the cylinder to be swung out for loading and ejecting the empty cases.
Cyclic rate	The rate of fire of an automatic weapon.
Cylinder	The cartridge container in a revolver.
Damascus	A damascus barrel is manufactured by the twisting of iron strips together then hammering them into one piece or strip. This strip is then hammer-welded round a mandril into a barrel. The outside of the barrel, when acid etched, shows the patterns of the twisted metal.
Delvigne	A breech system.
Derringer	Although this is the name of a specific manufacture, it is applied to all weapons of the small concealable pistol type.
Detonator	Usually applied to the device used to explode a powder charge.
Disc primer	A type of primer utilising a priming compound in a disc.
Disconnector	A part of the trigger that prevents two or more shots from being fired with a single pull of the trigger.
Double action	The use of the trigger on a revolver to both rotate the cylinder and to raise the hammer and let it drop.
Doubling	The failure of the disconnector to work thus letting the weapon fire more than one shot in this case two in succession.
Drift	The deviation of the bullet from its aimed path either caused by the wind, the rifling or gravity.
Drum magazine	A magazine that carries the cartridges in a drum shape.
Dry fire	The practice of firing a weapon without live ammunition.
Ducks foot	A weapon whose barrels diverge from the firing mechanism in the manner of a duck's foot.
Duelling pistol	A true duelling pistol was one of a pair and always exhibited the very best in the gunmaker's art.
Dumdum	A bullet with a soft nose that expands on impact. Outlawed by the Geneva Convention.
Dynamite	An explosive manufactured from nitroglycerine.
Effective range	The range that a bullet from a particular weapon can have a lethal effect.
Ejector	A device to throw the fired case clear of the weapon. This is often an integral part of the receiver.
Erosion	Damage caused to the barrel interior by the actions of the hot combustion gases.
Exterior ballistics	*See* Ballistics.
Extractor	A device for removing either an unfired or a fired round from the chamber of a weapon.
Extreme range	The maximum range that a particular weapon has any effect.
False muzzle	To stop any danger of the muzzle being worn on muzzle loaders and to stop the problem of loading a tight patched ball, a piece of barrel with a tapered bore was used to feed the ball into the real barrel.
Feed	The method in which a weapon has the cartridges delivered into it.
Field Strip	The stripping that is the minimum required to keep the weapon in battle condition.
Firing pin	A pin that detonates the cartridge priming.
Flechette	An ultra-small diameter projectile with a discarding sabot to enable it to be fired from a larger barrel. This gives an extremely high muzzle velocity and with the inherent instability of the long thin projectile the lethality is high.
Flare pistol	A pistol designed specifically to launch flares. Also called coloquially a Very pistol.
Flash hider or suppressor	A device fitted to the muzzle to lessen the muzzle flash on firing.
Flash hole	The hole in a cartridge or nipple that allows the flash from the primer or cap to reach the propellant.
Flash suppressant	A chemical added to the propellant to reduce the muzzle flash.
Flint	A type of stone used to cause the flash necessary to ignite the powder charge.
Flintlock	An ignition means that utilises a flint.
Fluted chamber	The difficulty of weapons using the delayed or straight blowback system and high power cartridges has led to the adoption of the fluted chamber. The flutes that run from the front of the chamber bleed some gas back along the sides of the case and thus float it clear of the chamber wall.
Follower	A follower as applied to the magazine is the part that, forced by the spring, follows the cartridges.
Fore end	The front part of the gripping surface under the barrel.
Foresight	A front sight.
Fouling	A deposit left in the barrel after firing. Can be powder derived or metallic from the bullet of its jacket.
Frame	The basic body of the weapon.
Gain twist	As applied to rifling, this is the type where the twist increases towards the muzzle of the weapon.
Gas check	As the velocity of a lead bullet is increased, the lead of the base tends to melt and the lead to be deposited on the walls of the bore. The gas check is of a harder metal and fixed to the base of the bullet to stop the melting. Also used when a gas seal is required during grenade launching.
Gas cylinder	The container for the gas piston on gas operated weapons.
Gas seal	As applied to a revolver, the gap between the cylinder is sealed at the moment of firing thus stopping the gas loss at the gap.
Gas system	Any system of operation of a weapon that uses gas tapped off from the barrel to operate the action.
Gauge	A system of bore measurement used mainly at present times for shotguns.
Gilding metal	An alloy used to cover bullet cores.
GPMG	General Purpose Machine Gun.
Grenade launcher	A weapon that is specifically designed to launch grenades, in a similar manner to a small mortar.
Grip (pistol grip)	The handle used to hold either a pistol or a similar type of grip used on a longarm.
Grip safety	A safety that is operated by the actual holding of the grip.
Groove	The part of the rifling that is cut out of the barrel.
Gun cotton	A type of propellant used normally in artillery.
Gunpowder	The first propellant and now known as black powder.
Gyrojet	A self-contained rocket of a comparable size to conventional ammunition.
Hair trigger	A trigger usually of the set type which has a particularly light firing pressure.
Half cock	A safety position in which the weapon cannot be fired, so called because the hammer is half-way between being fully down and cocked.
Half moon clip	On certain revolvers designed to fire rimmed cartridges a rimless cartridge can be fired when inserted in a special clip. This clip because of its shape being half a circle presents an appearance to that of the half-moon.
Hammer	A device to detonate the priming of a cartridge or actuate the firing pin.
Hammerless	A term applied to any weapon that does not employ a hammer in its operation. Often mistakenly applied to concealed hammer types.
Hammer spur	An extension on the hammer to facilitate the cocking of the weapon.
Hand Cannon	A hand held cannon ignition firearm.
Hand gun	Any weapon in the small arms class that can be fired from the hands. Present day usage limit it to pistols and revolvers.
Hang fire	Hang fire when applied to a firearm is when the weapon is fired and the cartridge and/or propellant does not ignite. In some cases this is only a delay and in others the cartridge never fires.
Harmonica gun	A pistol or rifle utilising a magazine that slides across the weapon at right angles to the vertical.
HE	High Explosive.
HEAT	High Explosive Anti-Tank.
Head space	The distance between the head of the cartridge and the face of the breech block or bolt. This is controlled by either a belt, a rim or a neck on the cartridge case.
HESH	High Explosive Squash Head.
Hesitation lock	A type of action that does not utilise a locked breech but by virtue of mechanical means allows a delay or hesitation in the opening of the breech.
Hinged barrel	A type of weapon in which the barrel hinges in any direction to permit loading.
HMG	Heavy Machine Gun.
Hold open	A device to hold the breech of a self-loading weapon open when the last shot has been fired.
Hollow point	Any bullet that has a hole in the point to assist expansion. Confined to sporting ammunition.
Holster	The container in which a pistol is carried by a person.
Incendiary	When applied to cartridges or grenades, the term describes the use of an inflammable filling usually self-igniting.
Inertia firing pin	A firing pin as a safety feature does not remain in contact with the primer but is held back by a spring. It therefore requires a full blow of the hammer to drive the pin forward and detonate the cartridge.
Inertia lock	Any type of lock that uses inertia to hold the breech closed.
Jacket	The covering used on a bullet or shell to either prevent a soft core from stripping or to protect the bore in the case of an armour-piercing core.

Jump	On firing, a bullet particularly in the case of the revolver, has to travel a short distance before encountering the rifling. This is signified by the term.
Keyhole	A bullet is said to keyhole when it strikes its target travelling sideways.
Kick	The colloquial term for recoil.
Kurz	The German description of a short rifle cartridge.
Land	The high point in the rifling of a barrel.
Leading	The depositing of lead in the barrel of a weapon from a lead bullet.
Lever action	A type of action typified by the Winchester weapon whereby the action is operated by a lever.
Leaf sight	A sight that employs as a means of elevation a strip of metal similar in operation to a hinge.
Live	A descriptive term applied to ammunition which is in its ready-to-fire state.
LMG	Light Machine Gun.
Load	A descriptive term applied to ammunition to designate the particular type and power.
Loading gate	A gate-like structure through which a weapon is loaded.
Lock	The lock mechanism of a gun is the part that connects the trigger to the hammer or striker.
Lock time	The time taken from the pulling of the trigger until the detonation of the cartridge.
Locking lug	A projection by which an action is locked.
Locked breech	Any breech system that has the bolt or breech lock positively attached to the chamber at the point of firing.
Magazine	As applied to small arms a container for the ammunition.
Magazine catch	The catch by which a removable magazine is held in place.
Magazine follower	The part of the magazine that imparts the pressure of the spring to the cartridges.
Magazine spring	The spring that forces the follower against the cartridges.
Magnum	A term, often misused, to denote a cartridge of higher power than normal.
Mainspring	The primary spring of a trigger mechanism.
Match	When applied to the matchlock this designates the means of ignition which is in the form of a slow match or burning chord.
Mechanical safety	Technically any safety that works by mechanical means but often used to differentiate between the safety catch and the grip safety.
Metal fouling	The jacketed bullet equivalent of leading, i.e. the depositing on the bore of a metallic residue.
MG	Machine Gun.
Miquelet	The Miquelet or Mediterranean lock is one that employs a massive external hammer spring with a combined frizzen and pan cover.
Misfire	The failure of a weapon to fire.
MMG	Medium Machine Gun.
Monopod	One-legged stand for a weapon.
Mushroom	A bullet is said to mushroom when it expands on impact. This often occurs in the shape of a mushroom.
Muzzle	The end of the barrel that the projectile emerges from.
Muzzle blast	The blast effect occurring at the muzzle on the firing of a weapon.
Muzzle brake	A device fitted to the muzzle of a weapon to reduce the recoil.
Muzzle energy	The energy that the bullet has by reason of its firing at the point of leaving the muzzle.
Muzzle flash	A flash occurring at the muzzle on firing.
Muzzle loader	Any weapon that is loaded from the muzzle end.
Muzzle velocity	The velocity of the bullet as measured at the muzzle of the weapon.
Neck	A part of the cartridge case usually of reduced diameter that the bullet is entered into, thus the expression 'to neck down a case' is to shorten the case by means of extending this portion.
Needle	The extended firing pin of a needle gun that passes through the propellant to reach the primer.
Night sight	A sight, either action (infra red) or passive (image intensifier) used for vision after dark.
Nitro-cellulose	An explosive formed by the action of nitric acid on cellulose.
Nitro-glycerine	An explosive formed by the action of nitric acid on glycerine.
Obturation	The sealing of the breech against the escape of gas achieved either by the expansion of the cartridge case or by a special sealing ring.
Open frame	The open frame type of revolver has no top strap and therefore lacks the strength of the fully framed weapon.
Open sight	A term synonymous with iron sights and used to denote a standard type of sight as opposed to telescopic.
Over and under	A weapon that has one barrel on top of another in a vertical plane.

Pan	The depression in which the priming powder is placed on the muzzle loading weapons.
Parabellum	The German word for War normally applied to either the Luger (p.08) pistol or the cartridge that it fires.
Parkerise	The protective finish applied to firearms normally of military nature.
Patch	A piece of material used to make the projectile grip the rifling and to reduce deposits in the bore.
Pellet, pill and patch lock	Lock systems utilising a priming compound contained in either pellets, pills or patches.
Pepper box	A revolving weapon in which the barrels and chambers are made as one and revolve as one.
Percussion cap	The cap shaped container of the priming compound on early, percussion weapons.
Pillar breech	A muzzle loading breech system that utilises a pillar in the centre of the barrel to deform the projectile into the rifling.
Pinfire	A type of cartridge or weapon to fire the cartridge that has as its means of priming a pin projecting from the cartridge case.
Pistol	A small firearm usually used with one hand.
Pitch	The degree of twist in the rifling of a barrel.
Point blank	Extremely short range.
Pressure	When applied to the breech of a gun it is the pressure generated by the burning of the propellant.
Primer	The container for the detonating compound.
Proof	An acceptance standard set by various countries to give a standard of safety in weapons.
Propellant	The substance that is burnt in a firearm to provide the gases to propel the projectile.
Pistol grip	A projection or grip on some gun stocks.
Pump gun	A type of repeating weapon that uses a pumping action to feed each cartridge. Also known as slide action.
Ramrod	A rod usually of wood used to force down the charge and projectile in a muzzle loaded weapon.
Ramp sight	A front sight which utilises a sloping ramp to allow the weapon to be drawn from a holster easily.
Rear sight	The element of the sight that is fitted nearest to the firer.
Rebound hammer	A hammer that does not in its normal position touch the primer.
Receiver	The main body of the weapon.
Recoil	The opposite force to that which propels the projectile.
Recoil lug	A projection which transmits the recoil either to the action of the weapon or to the stock.
Recoil operation	A weapon that utilises the force of the recoil to operate the self loading cycle.
Recoil spring	A main spring utilised to absorb the recoil and in many weapons to drive the breech block or slide into a firing position.
Recoil spring guide	A rod or tube that is used to prevent the recoil spring becoming damaged and in some cases to ease the stripping of the weapon.
Revolver	Any type of weapon that utilises a system incorporating a revolving element. Often taken to mean a revolving pistol as opposed to a self-loading one.
Ricochet	A ricochet is a projectile that skips off an object and continues in a different direction.
Rifling	Spiral grooves machined in the inside of a barrel to impart spinning motion to the projectile.
Rimfire	A cartridge that uses no separate primer but contains the priming compound in the rim of the case.
Rimless cartridge	A cartridge case that has no protruding rim.
Rpm	Rounds per minute.
Safety	A mechanical device to prevent the firing of a weapon.
Screw off barrel	A type of weapon that requires the barrel to be unscrewed for loading.
Selective fire	A weapon that can either be fired semi or fully automatically.
Selector	A means by which either semi or fully automatic fire can be chosen on a weapon.
Self loading	A term to describe a weapon that completes the ejection and reloading cycle by its own means.
Semi rim	A case with a partly protruding rim i.e. between rimless and rimmed.
Set trigger	A trigger that is set to fire by a separate lever. This is usually applied to a weapon that has an ultra light trigger.
Shaped charge	Usually applied to anti-tank weapons. This is the utilisation of a Munro effect which is the concentration of the effect of the explosive by shaping it.
Shot	Pellets of which a number are used at each discharge of a gun.
Side plate	A detachable plate allowing access to the mechanism of a weapon.

Side lock	A weapon where the lock extends rearward into the stock as opposed to the box lock in which the lock mechanism is contained forward of the stock.
Sight	Appliance attached to a firearm to allow precise aim.
Silencer	A device to reduce the noise of firing.
SL	Self loading.
Slide	Part of a self loading pistol which moves during the reloading cycle and contains the breech block.
Sling	A strap by which a weapon is carried.
Slow match	The means of igniting a cannon ignition or match lock weapon. Is usually a piece of thick chord possibly dipped in saltpetre.
SMG	Submachine Gun.
Smokeless powder	Any powder other than black powder. The name is derived from the fact that black powder produces dense smoke whereas the later propellants do not.
Smooth bore	An unrifled weapon.
Snaphance	A flint fired lock utilising a separate frizzen and pan cover.
Solid frame	Early revolvers featured no top strap and thus the frame is broken by a gap. A solid frame has a top strap.
Spur hammer	A hammer that has an extended spur to facilitate the cocking of the weapon.
Standing breech	A weapon that uses an immovable breech as opposed to the type that have the breech moving for loading.
Stock	The stock of a weapon is the part which provides the means of holding same.
Straight pull bolt	A straight pull bolt weapon does not require the bolt to be rotated when it is pulled rearward.
Submachine gun	An easily portable light recoil automatic weapon. Also known as a machine pistol.
Superimposed load	The loading of more than one charge, one on top of each other in a single barrel.
Swing out cylinder	A revolver in which the cylinder is swung sideways on a crane for loading and unloading.
Tape primer	A percussion system utilising the priming compound contained in a tape.
Teat fire	A percussion system utilising the priming compound contained in a teat.
Throat	The part of the barrel between the end of the chamber and the beginning of the rifling.
Toggle action	A recoil system utilising a toggle joint.
Top strap	The part of a solid frame revolver which joins the top of the standing breech to the top of the barrel.
Touch hole	The hole on a muzzle loading weapon through which the propellant is ignited.
Trajectory	The path of a projectile from the moment of firing until its impact with its target.
Trigger	A lever by which the firing mechanism is actuated.
Trigger guard	A guard fitted round the trigger to stop accidental firing.
Trigger stop	A means of arresting the travel of the trigger after firing.
Twist	The spiral of the rifling.
Tube lock	A percussion system utilising the priming compound contained in a tube.
Under hammer	A weapon that uses a hammer on the underside of the action.
Velocity	The speed of a bullet.
Volley gun	A weapon that fires more than one shot simultaneously.
Wadcutter	A flat-nosed bullet usually used in target shooting.
WCF	Winchester Centre Fire.
Wheellock	A lock system that utilises a spinning wheel to strike the flint thus causing the spark for ignition.
Windage	The amount of sight deviation required in a horizontal plane.
WRF	Winchester Rimfire.
Zero	Used as 'to zero a gun' means that a mean sight position is arrived at.

APPENDIX 'C'

A list of some of the available Reference Works. Author

Mauser, Walther and Mannlicher Firearms	*Smith*
Forsyth & Co Patent Gunmakers	*W. Keith Neal*
Automatic Pistols	*Pollard*
Treatise on Military Small Arms and Ammunition 1888	
Patent Specifications relating to Firearms 1588–1858	
A History of Spanish Firearms	*James D. Lavin*
Early Percussion Firearms	*Louis Winant*
Revolving Arms	*A. W. F. Talerson*
The Mantons: Gunmakers	{ *W. Keith Neal* / *D. H. L. Black*
Remington Arms	*Alden Hatch*
The Art of the Gunmaker Vols I & II	*J. F. Hayward*
The Book of Colt Firearms	*R. Q. Sutherland*
Colt Firearms from 1836	*R. L. Wilson*
Guns and Rifles of the World	*Severn Blackmore*
Guns	*Dudley Pope*
One Hundred Great Guns	*Merrill Lindsay*
The Winchester Book	*Madis*
The Mauser Self-Loading Pistol	*Bedford & Dunlop*
System Mauser	*B. Schroeder*
Pistol and Revolver Cartridges	*White & Marshall*
Military Pistols and Revolvers	*Hogg*
Small Arms	*Wilkinson*
A Dictionary of Modern War	*Edward Ludwark*
Infantry Weapons	*John Weeks*
German Infantry Weapons of World War II	*Barker*
Russian Infantry Weapons	*Barker & Walter*
British and American Infantry Weapons of World War II	*Barker*
Guide to United States Machine Guns	*Konrad Schreider*
Japanese Infantry Weapons	*Normount*
German Infantry Weapons	*Normount*
German Pistols and Holsters 1934/1945	*Whittington*
The Book of Pistols and Revolvers	*Smith*
The Book of Rifles	*Smith*
The Lee Enfield Rifle	*E. G. B. Reynolds*
The Luger Pistol	*F. Datrig*
Smith and Wesson	*Neil & Jinks*
Encyclopaedia of Firearms	*M. Petersen*
Cartridges of the World	*F. Barnes*
Pepperbox Firearms	*J. Dunlop*
The Gatling Gun (Herbert Jenkins London)	*Wahl & Toppol*
Confederate Handguns	*Fuller*
European Hand Firearms	*Jackson & Whitelaw*
The Webley Story	*Dowell*
The World's Submachine Guns	*Nelson*
The Handgun	*Boothroyd*
Bolt Action Rifles	*F. de Haas*
Small Arms of the World	*Smith & Smith*
The World's Assault Rifles	*Musgrave & Nelson*
German Machine Guns	*Musgrave & Oliver*
The Revolver 1818–1865 : 1865–1888 : 1888–1914	*Taylerson*
Game Guns and Rifles	*Akehurst*
The Pictorial History of the Machine Gun	*F. Hobart*

ANNUALS
Gun Digest
Guns and Ammo Annual

MONTHLY OR WEEKLY
Guns Review
Shooting Times
Guns and Ammo
American Rifleman
Small Arms Profile

Chapter 7

Weapons in Close Up

This section is devoted to the close study of a number of different weapons in four groups: Pistols, Rifles, Submachine Gun, and Machine Gun. These weapons show the changing methods of construction and the evolvement of the type.

The Short Barrelled Sea Service Flintlock Pistol

The Short Sea Service Pistol was issued during the reign of George III. A particular example illustrated was manufactured about 1800. The early version of which this is one has a 9″ barrel with a 24 bore. The ramrod was of brass tipped wood, this was rapidly replaced for durability by a steel rod and for dependability attached by a swivel to the front of the barrel. The bore is the same as the Long Barrelled Sea Service Pistol and was rapidly changed to a 16 bore when it was then known as the Carbine bore pistol.

The pistol is fully wooden stocked. The brass butt cap is retained by a single screw. The trigger guard is also of brass and being quite ornate in design. The ramrod guide and holder are also of brass inlet into the fore-end. The lock retaining plate on the left side of the pistol is of plain brass. Also fitted to the left side of the pistol is a steel belt hook which enables the pistol to be hung from the belt without the use of a holster. The lock is of simple construction but being large enough to be durable in service. The lock is marked 'Tower' and further forward a Crown over the letters GR.

The barrel plug has an extension that is retained with a single screw into the top of the butt. This pistol is typical of the simple well constructed military flintlock.

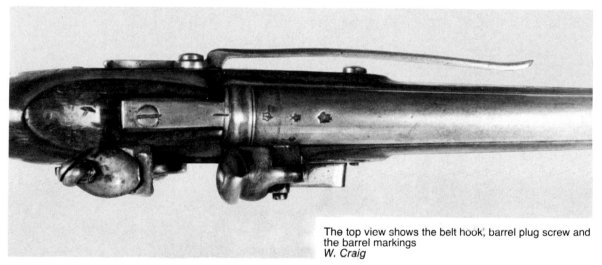

The top view shows the belt hook, barrel plug screw and the barrel markings
W. Craig

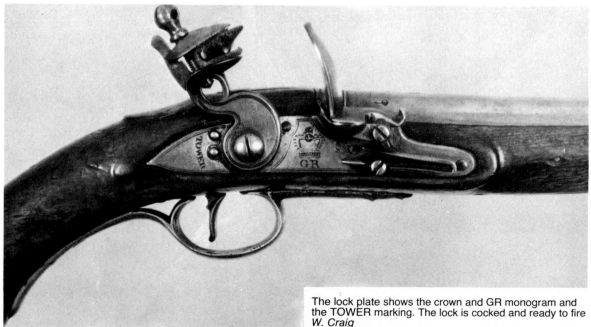

The lock plate shows the crown and GR monogram and the TOWER marking. The lock is cocked and ready to fire
W. Craig

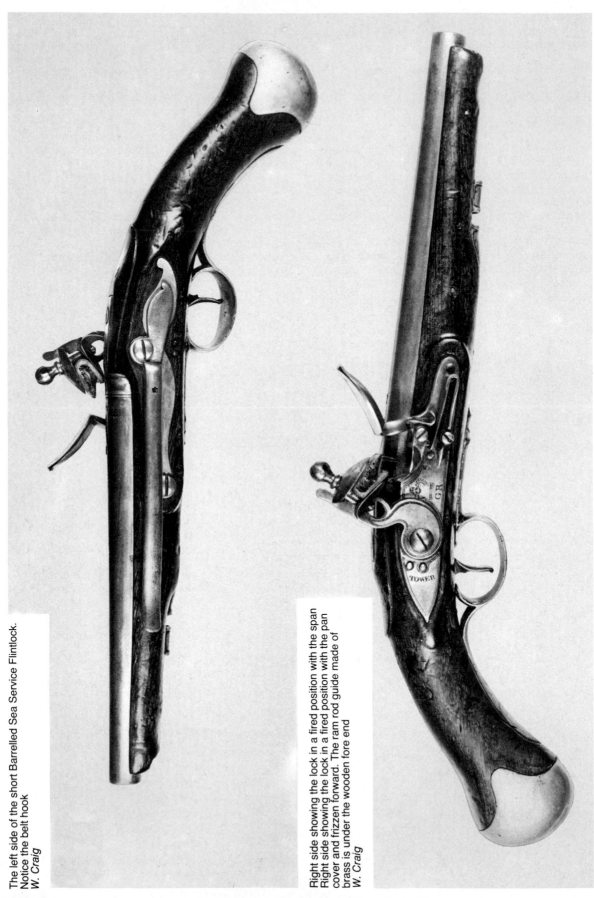

The left side of the short Barrelled Sea Service Flintlock.
Notice the belt hook
W. Craig

Right side showing the lock in a fired position with the span
Right side showing the lock in a fired position with the pan
cover and frizzen forward. The ram rod guide made of
brass is under the wooden fore end
W. Craig

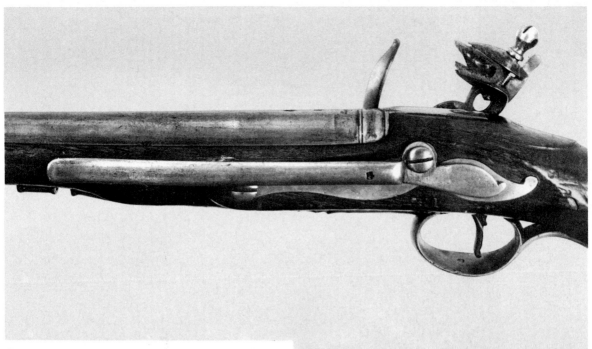

Close up of the belt hook used for carrying the pistol through the belt. The hook is bolted to the side plate which is made of brass
W. Craig

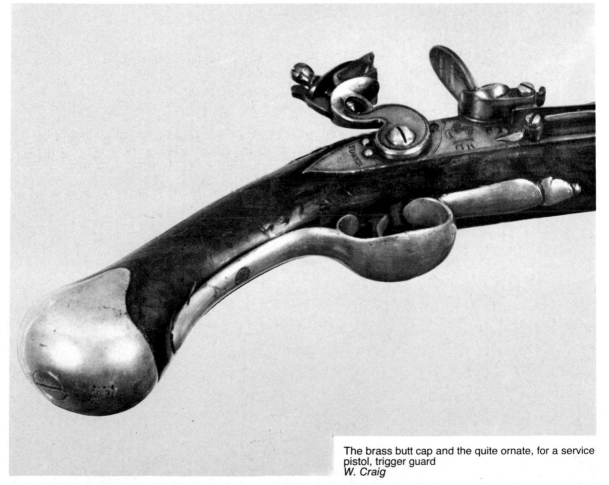

The brass butt cap and the quite ornate, for a service pistol, trigger guard
W. Craig

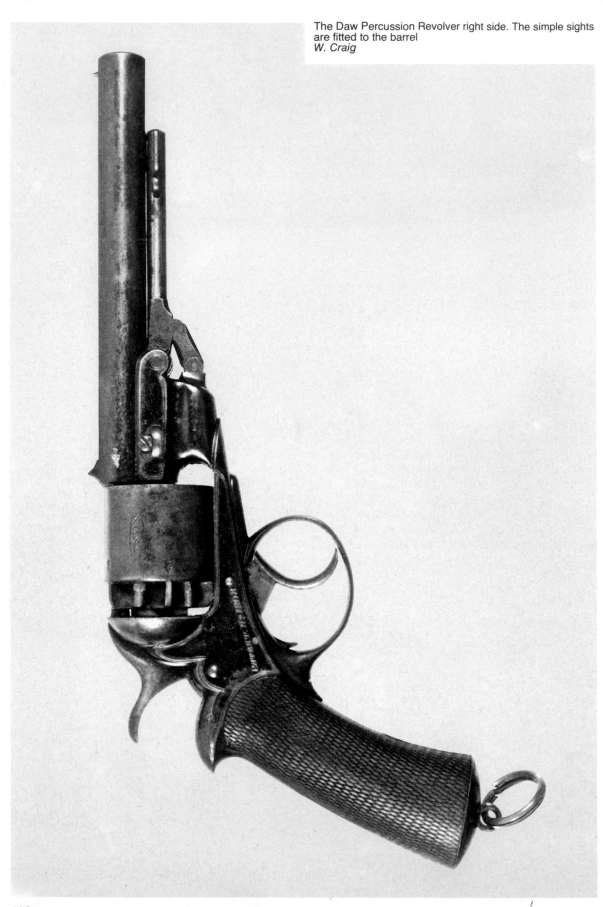

The barrel markings 'GEORGE H. DAW, 57 THREADNEEDLE STREET, LONDON. PATENT NO. 1808.'
Author

The left side showing the double action trigger, ramrod and the lanyard ring on the butt cap
Author

Daws Percussion Revolver

George Henry Daw was a designer who worked on both pistols and cartridges. In his latter days he worked from 57 Threadneedle Street, London, having moved there in about 1851 as Witton, Daw & Co. His own company became known as George Henry Daw in 1860. Although Daw used the patents of Pryse and Cashmore for certain components such as the rammer, the capping system was his own.

Problems were experienced with all percussion revolvers with the percussion caps which could fall off and jam the weapon, or even detonate when the weapon was dropped on to them. The advantage of the Daws design was that the caps were positioned through a U shaped notch in the recoil shield on the top of the weapon. This gap allowed for easy loading but was closed entirely by the hammer when it was down. This meant that the caps were held in place by the recoil shield during rotation and during firing, the firer is shielded from the cap completely. As there was no gap for a cap to be hit

the weapon was completely safe at all times. Daw was a clever promoter and managed to persuade General Garibaldi to accept two of his revolvers. Garibaldi is said to have remarked on the simplicity of the system. The price of a typical pistol in 1860 was from £6.10 up to £10.00.

The pistol illustrated is a five shot three-quarter 80 bore with a barrel length of 5¾in (145mm). The rifling is five groove with a right hand twist. It is retained in a similar manner to the Colt type crosskey with a retaining screw. The serial number that is placed both on the right of the cylinder frame and on the top of the barrel is 1808. This could be confused with a patent number owing to the markings but on other pistols the number is in the same position and varies. The sights are a simple post foresight with a V groove machined in an integral block on the rear of the barrel. The rammer mechanism is simply activated by depressing a catch on the side of the lever and pulling down. The grips are of finely chequered wood and a lanyard ring is fitted to the base of the butt.

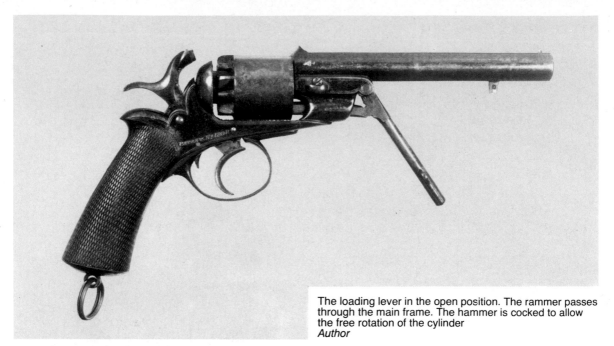

The loading lever in the open position. The rammer passes through the main frame. The hammer is cocked to allow the free rotation of the cylinder
Author

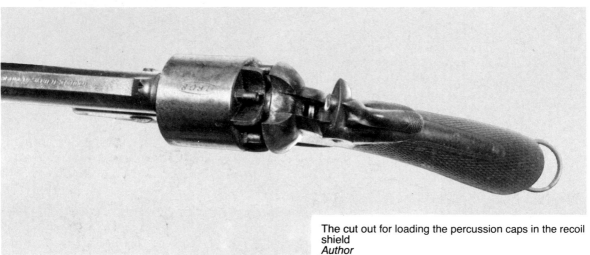

The cut out for loading the percussion caps in the recoil shield
Author

Webley Fosbery

At the beginning of the twentieth century there were a number of challengers such as the Luger, the Mauser 1896 and Colt to the well-established revolver, Colonel G. Vincent Fosbery, V.C., decided that it was possible to combine the best features of a revolver with a self loading pistol. The resultant weapon was announced in 1901 and put on sale. It was in effect a recoil operated revolver based on the standard Webley ·455 Service Revolver.

Although it was never adopted officially as a Service weapon many were carried by officers during World War I. Production of the Webley Fosbery ceased about the time of the end of the War.

The 1902 Target Model was typical of the final design and was fitted with a 7½in barrel. The normal barrel lengths encountered are 4in, 6in and 7½in. A safety catch is fitted on the left side and is pushed upward to put on 'safe' at which time a

brass plate with the word 'safe' becomes visible. The weapon is loaded in a similar way to all break-frame Webley revolvers. After loading the hammer is cocked by hand, upon which the weapon is ready for firing. On firing the recoil energy moves the barrel and cylinder approximately ¾in. This movement cocks the hammer and a fixed stud in the bottom half of the frame forces the cylinder to rotate one-twelfth of a turn. The return spring drives the barrel and cylinder back approximately ¾in. This the cylinder a further one-twelfth thereby lining up a new cartridge. The foresight is a removable blade with different blades being fitted for different ranges. The rear sight is adjustable for direction by forcing across in its groove. The weapon is marked on the top of the barrel P. Webley & Son, London & Birmingham. On the left side of the frame Webley-Fosbery and 455 Cordite along with Webely's winged bullet insignia.

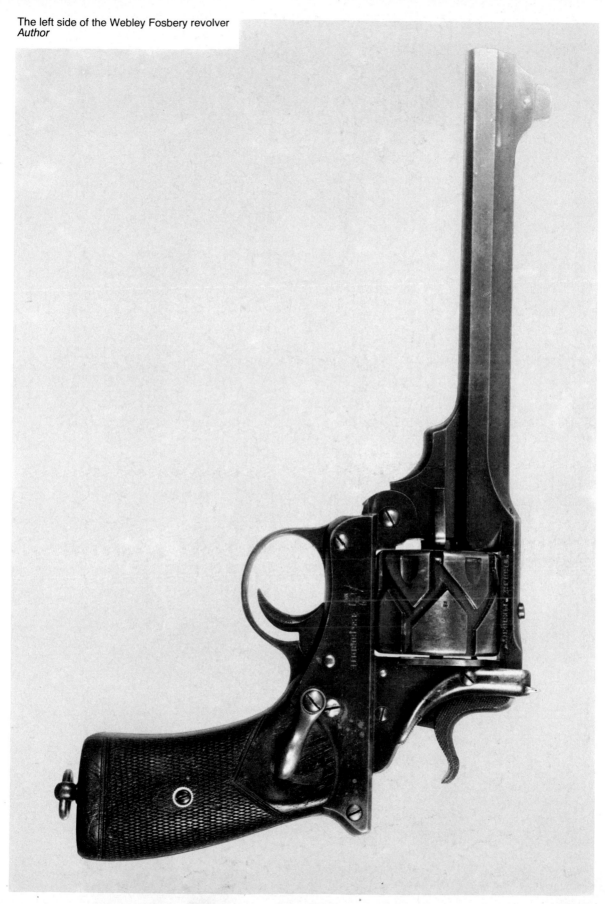

The left side of the Webley Fosbery revolver
Author

The zig-zag cylinder grooves provide the rotation. The
barrel catch also carries the rear sight
Author

The safety applied and the weapon cocked. The legend
SAFETY is brass
Author

The cartridges in the process of extraction
Author

The revolver open with the extraction and ejection complete. The stud which rotates the cylinder is visible on the main frame just forward of the recoil shield
Author

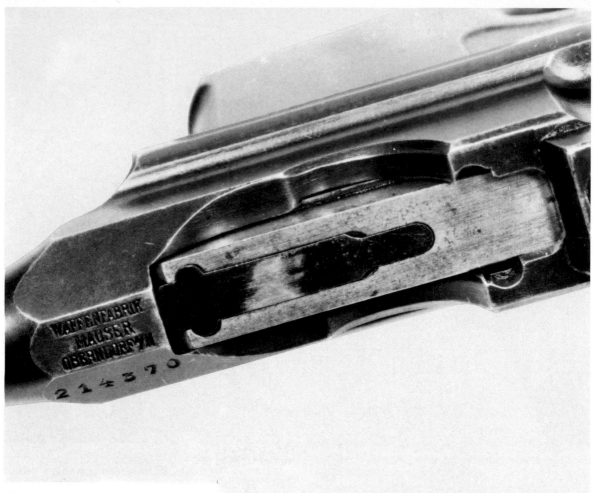

The bolt top with the later type of extractor
Author

The Mauser 1896

Paul and Wilhelm Mauser set up a small factory at Oberndorf and when the chance to purchase a Government factory with financial help came up they branched out. When his brother died in 1882 Paul was left in sole charge and in 1884 changed the name of the factory to Waffenfabrik Mauser. In 1887 for one reason or another, possibly financial, Paul sold a controlling interest in the factory to Ludwick Loewe and became the superintendent of the design department. During the period 1893–94 he worked on a pistol that was to become the Mauser 1896. The firm was finally taken over by DWM. The Mauser 1896 was produced with few mechanical changes throughout its life. The only major changes were the use of multiple locking lugs on the bolt after the intitial production batch (the original loading of the Mauser 7·63mm was lighter than the final version). The extractor was changed in shape, the firing pin had an extra lug added and the trigger and safety catch were changed in their methods of operation. Externally there were changes in barrel length, hammer shape, grip shape, magazine capacity and sights. Unlike some of its contemporaries the Mauser did not become a

military success but remained a commercial weapon. The Broomhandle as it is often known from its distinctive outline served through both world wars and such illustrious people as Sir Winston Churchill chose it. A fully automatic selectable fire version was manufactured and known as the Schnellfeuer. Most of the pistols were manufactured to take a shoulder stock that could double as a holster. The pistol is recoil operated. The upper receiver slides in the lower on recoil forcing the locking block to be pulled down out of engagement with the bolt and allowing the bolt to move rearward. The machining of the components is unusually complex as no pins are used as pivots and the pivots are machined as part of the components. The weapon is clip loaded with a stripper clip into a box magazine machined integrally with the frame. The normal load is ten rounds. The complete hammer and locking mecahnism can be removed in a group from the lower receiver. The Mauser is hammer-fired with the long firing pin being contained in the bolt. The extractor is fitted in the top of the bolt and the ejector which is fitted into the body slides through a slot in the lower side of the bolt.

The bolt to the rear showing the lock lugs
Author

The fitting pin is slotted so that it can be removed. The hammer is cocked and the safety is in the fire position. The stripping latch is at the top of the back strap
Author

The Mauser 1896 pistol left side
Author

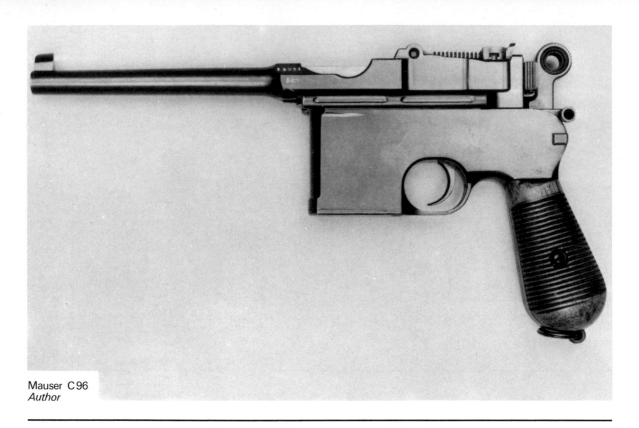

Mauser C 96
Author

The pistol is unusual in that it is clip-loaded in the manner of a rifle
Author

The distances marked in meters on the rear sight may be a bit optimistic for a low powered pistol cartridge even if the weapon was fitted with the shoulder stock
Author

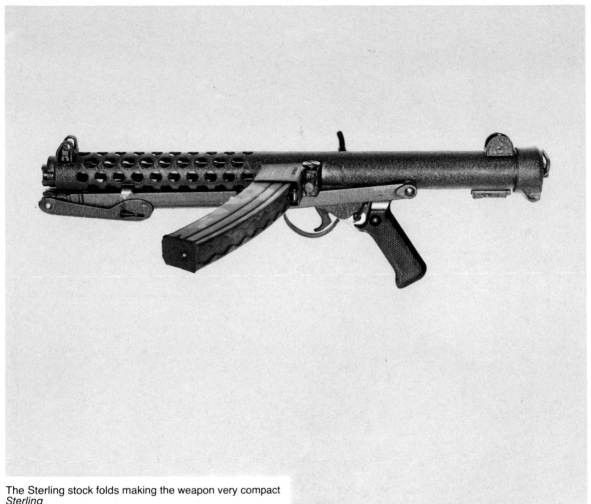

The Sterling stock folds making the weapon very compact
Sterling

The Sterling Sub Machine Gun

After World War I, G. H. Lanchester who was working for the Sterling Engineering Co. developed a sub machine gun closely modelled on the German MP.28. During the early part of World War II about one hundred thousand were produced primarily for the Royal navy. In 1942 a new weapon designed by G. W. Patchet was developed and tested. By 1944 the new submachine gun was ready for limited production and some were made before the end of the war.

During post war trials held in 1947 there were a number of entries including the Patchet, BSA and Madsen. The Patchet experienced trouble with the trigger, other contestants also experienced a variety of faults. By a trial held in 1951 the Patchet was held to be the best and particularly good in the mud test and in the stripping test. BSA not convinced that their entry had had a fair trial insisted on another test in 1952 at which the Patchet was confirmed the winner.

The Patchet was approved for service on September 18th 1953 as the L2A1. This mark was declared obsolete in April 1955 and the L2A2 adopted for only one month when the L2A3 became the standard weapon. This mark is still manufactured today by the Sterling Armament Co. and is better known as the Sterling. A silenced version is also produced under Patchet patent and is known as the L34A1. The total production is not known but as the MoD produced 163500 and the Sterling production is in six figures it is considerable. The Sterling is constructed from a prepunched steel tube body on to which a number of components are brazed. The major ones are the magazine well and pistol grip/trigger mount. The barrel is fitted through the body and held in place by two Allen screws at the muzzle. The ejector is fixed to the body at the rear of the magazine well and held in place by an Allen screw. The magazine release passes through the ejector. The bolt has a fixed firing pin and a spring-loaded extractor. The return spring is double and is fitted into a well in the bolt. An ejector slot and feed guides are machined into the bolt and helical dirt grooves are machined round the exterior. The cocking handle fits through a slot in the body and is held by a spring-loaded plunger and the return spring cap. The back cap is a bayonet fit and doubles as a catch for the folding stock. The trigger unit is removable by the turning of a cross pin 90 degrees. Selective fire is normal but a single shot trigger is available for police use.

The Sterling-Patchet silenced submachine gun
Sterling

The bolt face shows the fixed firing pin machined on to it. The extractor is not fitted but the slot for the ejector is on the right side between the feed slots
Author

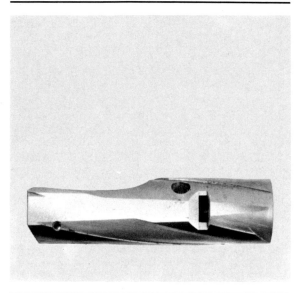

The lower side of the bolt showing the ejector slots and the feed slots. Notice the helical dirt grooves machined into the external face
Author

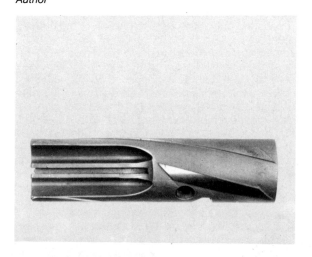

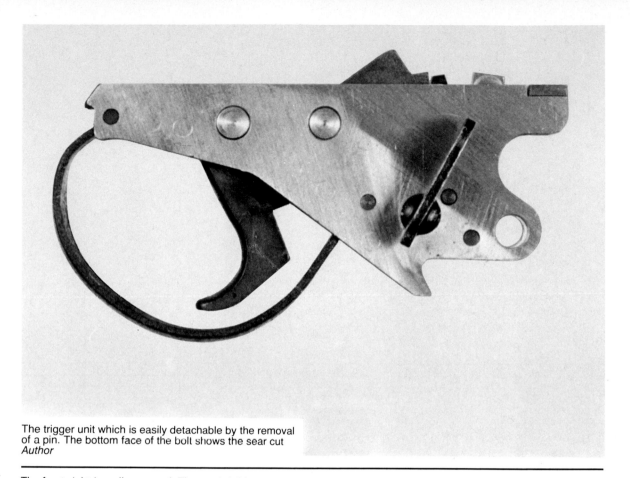

The trigger unit which is easily detachable by the removal of a pin. The bottom face of the bolt shows the sear cut
Author

The front sight is well protected. The stock folds and clips into the barrel jacket
Author

The magazine well and release
Sterling

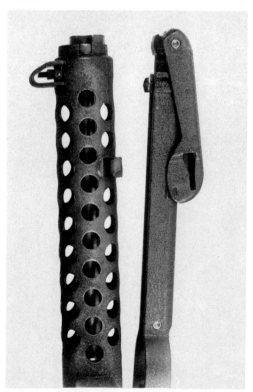

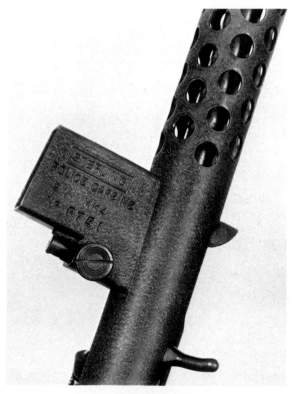

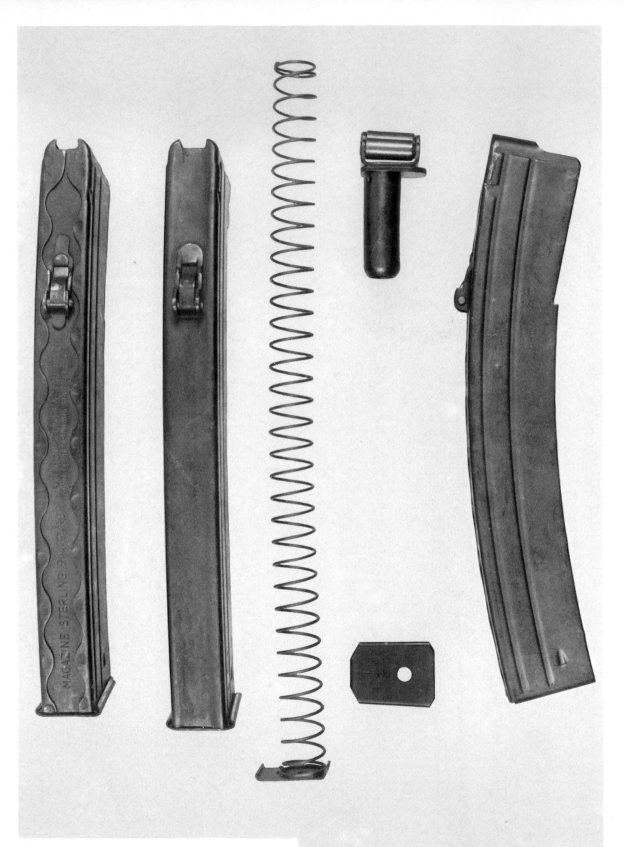

The magazine strips easily for cleaning. The cartridge
follower is a roller type giving reliable feed. The left hand
magazine is the standard production type welded from
pressings, the right hand is a solid tube bent to shape
Author

The Sterling submachine gun fitted with a bayonet and with the stock extended and a magazine fitted
Sterling

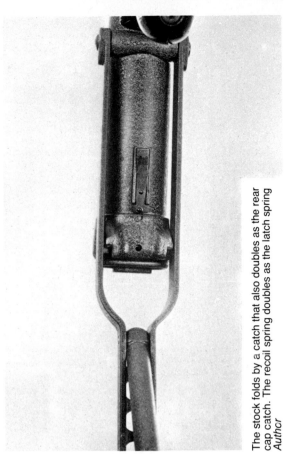

The stock folds by a catch that also doubles as the rear cap catch. The recoil spring doubles as the latch spring
Author

The bayonet lug is welded to the body on the left. The hand is protected at both muzzle and ejection slot by welded on guards
Author

The Snider-Enfield Carbine
Author

The breech catch on the later weapons was improved and has to be pressed in to lift the cover and withdraw the catch at the rear of the breech. The SNIDER PATENT legend is on the breech block
Author

The Snider-Enfield

With the introduction of a breech loading needle gun by the Prussians in their war with the Dutch, other governments decided the days of the muzzle loader were numbered.

In August 1864 the British government announced that they would welcome designs for the conversion of the existing muzzleloader into a breech loader. Surprisingly about fifty entries were received. While most were still percussion fired one was cartridge firing. This conversion was the work of Jacob Snider and by 1865 it had been accepted as the official conversion of the Enfield muzzle loader. The final development that was to make the venture a success was the development of a suitable cartridge by Col. Edward Boxer in 1866. The conversion was carried out by substituting a new breech end to the existing barrel. The weapon was known as the Snider Enfield. When the last of the muzzle loaders had been converted a weapon was manufactured

This weapon was made by the London Arms Company LAC is 1862. The crown and VR initials are at the rer of the lock plate
Author

The brass butt trap open. Unit markings are on the top along with the WD and arrow stamp
Author

from scratch using a steel barrel with five groove Enfield rifling and a modified breech lock. This rifle was known as the Mark III.

The Snider Enfield was produced in two versions—a long barrelled rifle and a short barrelled carbine.

The Mark III Cavalry Carbine was a well constructed weapon having the previously mentioned steel barrel with extra locking on the breech. The catch on the left of the breech block is depressed and the breech block swung over on a hinge pin which is on the right of the receiver. The cartridge can then be placed in the breech and chambered by hand. The breech block is then swung closed. To extract the fired cartridge the breech block is swung open and pulled to the rear causing the extractor to pull out the empty case. This is an extremely simple but effective solution for the conversion of a muzzle loader. The butt plate and trigger guard are brass and on the carbine version the wooden fore-end extends only part of the way forward. The weapon has a fixed foresight and the rear sight may be folded upwards when it then becomes adjustable by sliding up a blade.

The weapon ready to fire and the leaf rear sight raised
Author

The breech open and a cartridge being extracted
Author

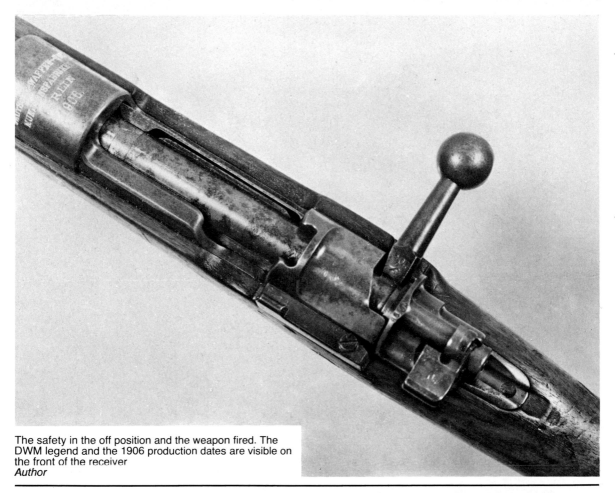

The safety in the off position and the weapon fired. The DWM legend and the 1906 production dates are visible on the front of the receiver
Author

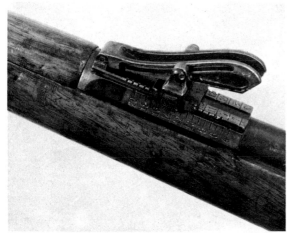

The rear sight is a complicated cam adjusted tangent type. It is adjustable to 2000 meters
Author

Infanteriegewehr M.98

The history of the Mauser factory has been told under the Mauser 1896 pistol. In 1872 Mauser brothers were given an order for 100,000 Mod '71 rifles and from that time on the factory turned out a continual flow of rifles and at the same time introduced modifications. It was not until the adoption of the Model 1898 on 5th April of that year that the finite design emerged. The rifle was chambered for the M 1888 cartridge initially but was modified in 1903 to the M 1898. While both are known as 7·92mm Mauser cartridges the latter type has a larger diameter bullet. By 1904 a number of countries adopted the M98 and by the outbreak of war the weapon was in full production for the German Army including a shortened version known as the Kar.98.

The M.98 is a turn bolt rifle with two locking lugs at the front of the bolt that lock into the barrel extension and a third safety lug at the rear that locks into the receiver bridge. The weapon cocks on the closing of the bolt which has a straight handle. The bolt is removed from the rifle by pulling out a catch at the left of the receiver bridge and drawing it to the rear. Unusually the bolt will close on an empty chamber which does not let the soldier know when the weapon is empty. This was later modified as a result of experience at the beginning of World War I. The sights are a simple blade foresight and a tangent rear sight which is marked to 2000 metres. The bayonet lug is on the underside of the barrel and also has an opening for a cleaning rod. There is also on the front barrel band a stacking hook. The safety catch is on the rear of the bolt and operates by flipping the lever through 180 degrees.

The Model 1898 is the basis for all modern Mauser actions and there is very little change even today.

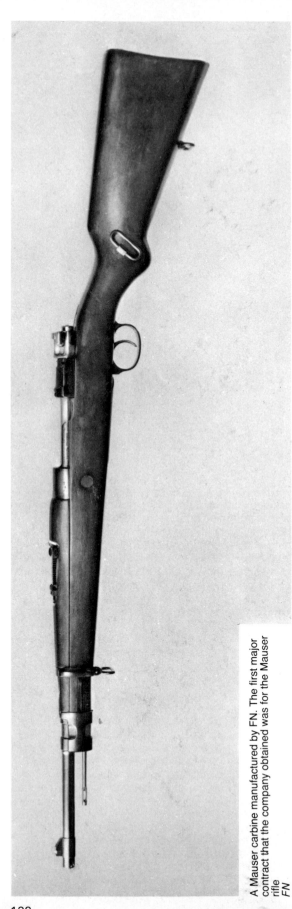

A Mauser carbine manufactured by FN. The first major contract that the company obtained was for the Mauser rifle
FN

The bayonet fitting on the Mauser '98
Author

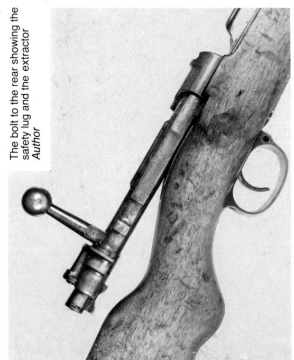

The bolt to the rear showing the safety lug and the extractor
Author

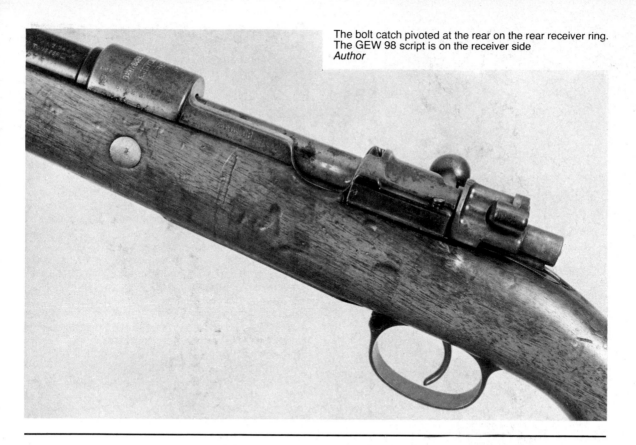

The bolt catch pivoted at the rear on the rear receiver ring. The GEW 98 script is on the receiver side
Author

The safety is in the safe position and the weapon cocked. The bolt is removed by the pulling out of the lever on the left rear of the receiver
Author

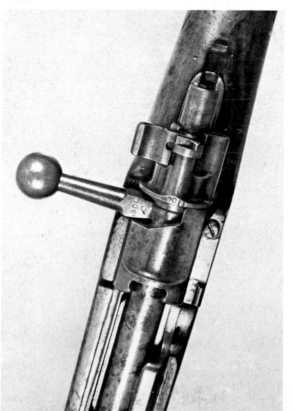

With the bolt removed the magazine platform and clip guide are visible
Author

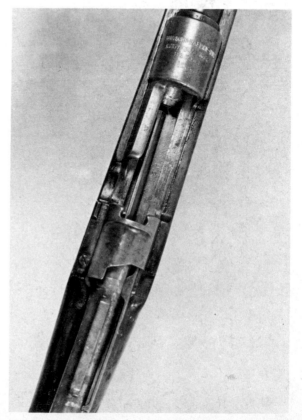

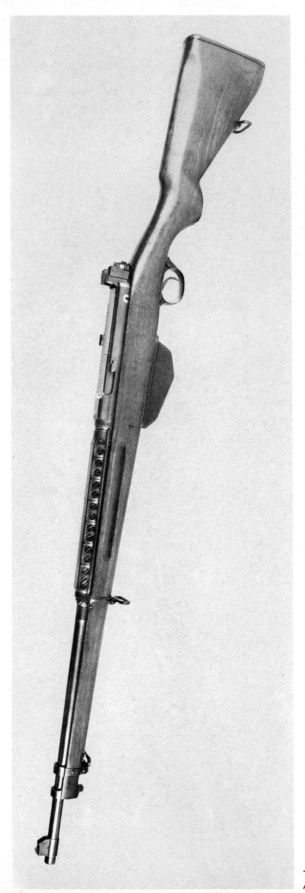

The Vickers Pedersen

The Pedersen rifle is unusual not only in its method of operation but also in that it was designed and produced in the 1920s. J. D. Pedersen went to work for the American government arsenal at Springfield. His brief was to design a new rifle and what is unusual he was also allowed to design a cartridge along with it. The cartridge was the ·276 Pedersen which was claimed to have superior ballistics to most cartridges of that time while being 25 percent lighter. The cartridge was adopted for the American weapon test in 1929 but the immense cost of a change in calibre made the government stick to the tested 30-06. The rifle failed unfortunately, probably because the ammunition for it had to be lubricated for reliable operation.

The weapon works by a cleverly conceived hesitation lock but as with all blowback weapons the bolt begins to move at the instant of firing and as a result, with the high powered cartridge, there were troubles with the cartridge heads separating on ejection. The weapon is beautifully constructed of high grade materials and has a well finished wooden stock and fore-end with cooling vents in the underside. The top cover is metal with multiple cooling apertures. The loading clip is like the Garand contained in the rifle and only ejected when the weapon is empty. It contains ten rounds. The barrel exterior is on the rear portion machined with helical cooling grooves and is fully floating. The extractor is on the top of the bolt face and the ejector is a spring loaded pin on the left of the face. The delay operates in a similar manner to a Luger or Vickers toggle but being blowback operated has no cam to break the joint. Instead the joint is broken by the rearward pressure and relies on the clever cam in closed position long enough for the pressure to drop to an acceptable level for ejection. The lack of a slow initial extraction led Pedersen to develop a dry wax lubricant for the bullets to help them slide along the chamber walls when the pressure was high. The sights are a simple post foresight with a complicated drum operated adjustable rear aperture. The trigger mechanism is removable as a group.

The Vickers-Pedersen
Author

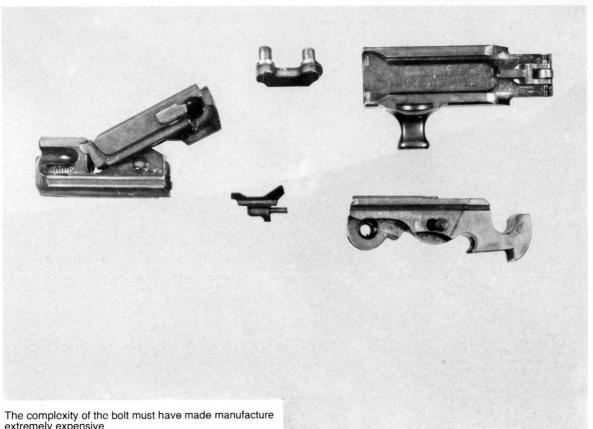

The complexity of the bolt must have made manufacture
extremely expensive
Author

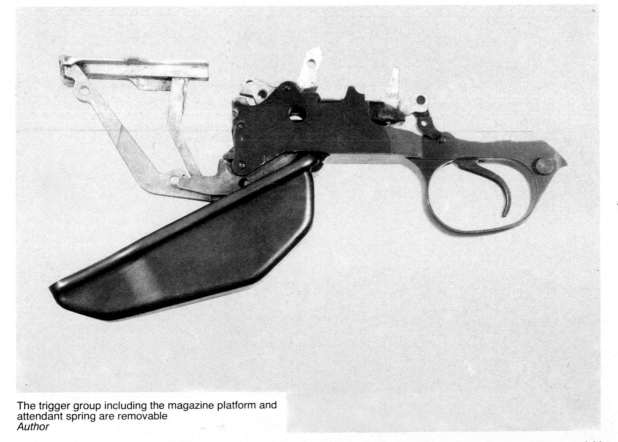

The trigger group including the magazine platform and
attendant spring are removable
Author

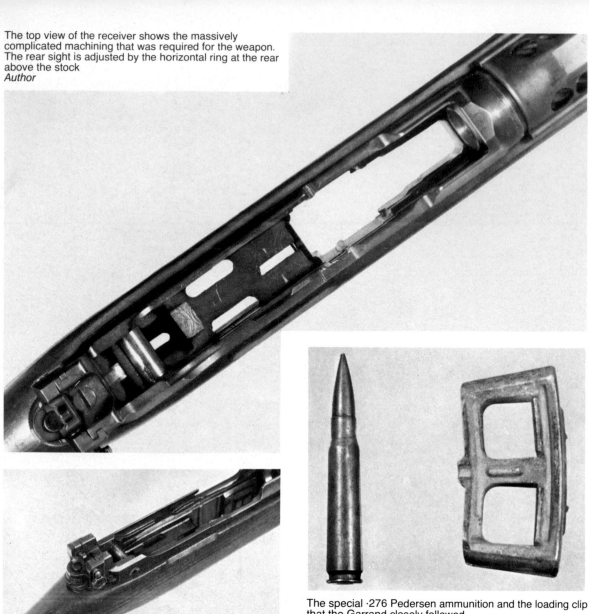

The top view of the receiver shows the massively complicated machining that was required for the weapon. The rear sight is adjusted by the horizontal ring at the rear above the stock
Author

The special ·276 Pedersen ammunition and the loading clip that the Garrand closely followed
Author

The complex rear sight that is adjustable for elevation and driection. The main pivot pin for the toggle passes through the main receiver
Author

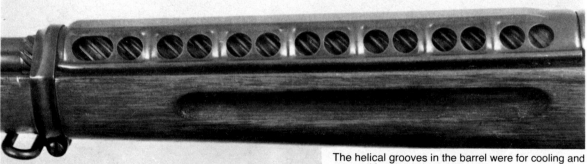

The helical grooves in the barrel were for cooling and covered by a metal pressing
Author

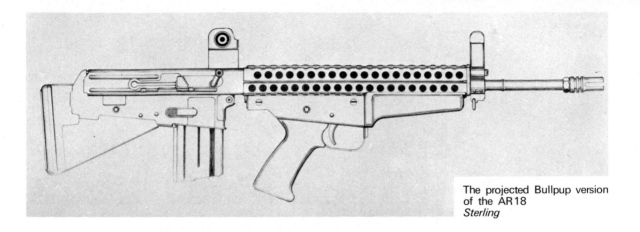

The projected Bullpup version
of the AR18
Sterling

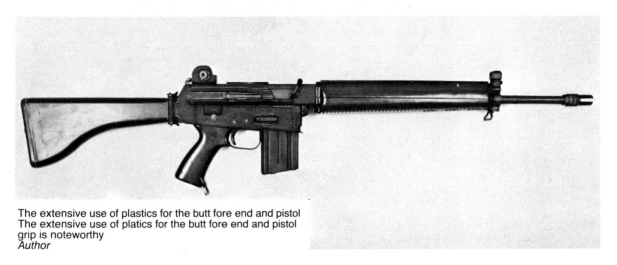

The extensive use of plastics for the butt fore end and pistol
The extensive use of platics for the butt fore end and pistol
grip is noteworthy
Author

The Sterling/Armalite AR18

When the Armalite company was originally formed it
was with private capital. In 1954 it became part of
the Fairchild Engine and Aeroplane Corp. and
devoted itself to the development of military
weapons. After a number of projects the company
decided to employ Eugene Stoner in 1954. Stoner is
one of the best firearms designers of the post war
era.

While it was accepted that major military powers
have massive production capacity there was,
Armalite felt, a gap for a weapon that would be easy
to produce by the less sophisticated nations. The
weapon designed was the AR16 which appeared in
1959–60. The AR16 was chambered for the then
popular 7·62mm NATO round and was extremely
simple in manufacture and construction.
Unfortunately the interest turned to small calibre
weapons and the weapon was not adopted.
After Stoner had left the company a rifle, the AR18,
was designed. This was very closely modelled on
the AR16 but was chambered for the 5·56mm
cartridge. Lacking production facilities themselves
Armalite arranged for the AR18 to be produced in
Japan by the Howa Machinery Company of Nagoya.
A small number of AR18s and some single shot
AR180s were produced before Armalite ended the
agreement and decided to produce the weapons
themselves. The well known firm of Sterling
Armament of England were, in the early '70s
engaged in an exercise to produce a small calibre
military rifle and purchased the complete production
package from Armalite. The weapon was in
production in AR18, AR18S and AR180 versions by
1976.

The AT18 is constructed from two major pressings
which form the upper and lower receivers and
which pivot for stripping. The barrel is threaded into
a barrel extension that is welded into the upper
receiver and the pistol grip and folding stock are
mounted on to the lower. The pistol grip, stock,
lower and upper hand guards are manufactured
from plastic. The front sight is carried on a block
mounted on the barrel and which also carries the
gas piston.

The weapon functions by the hammer striking the
firing pin which detonates the primer. When the
bullet passes the gas port in the barrel, gas is fed
up through the front site block where it drives a
piston to the rear which in turn moves a rod into
contact with the bolt. The bolt moves rearward and
a cam slot turns the bolt head out of engagement
with the barrel extension and allows the complete
bolt to move to the rear. The extractor and the pin
type ejector are carried in the bolt head.

The main fire selector and safety is fitted on the left of the weapon. Note the hinge for the folding stock
Author

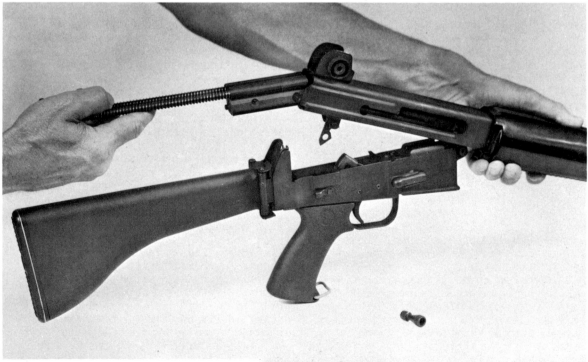

The AR18 is easy to strip into its major components
Sterling

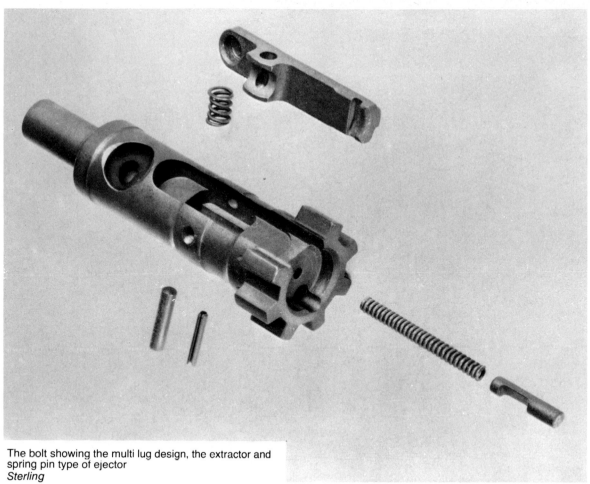

The bolt showing the multi lug design, the extractor and
spring pin type of ejector
Sterling

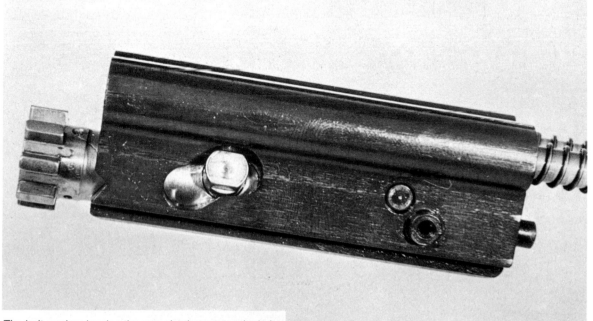

The bolt carrier showing the cam slot that rotates the bolt
for locking and unlocking. The recoil springs are mounted
on the bolt guide rods
Author

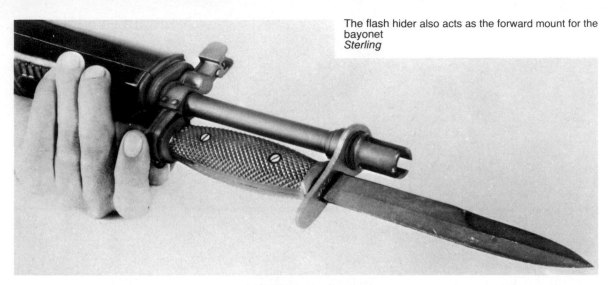

The flash hider also acts as the forward mount for the bayonet
Sterling

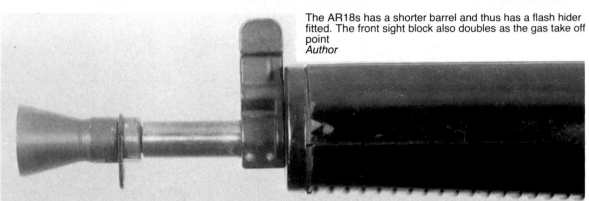

The AR18s has a shorter barrel and thus has a flash hider fitted. The front sight block also doubles as the gas take off point
Author

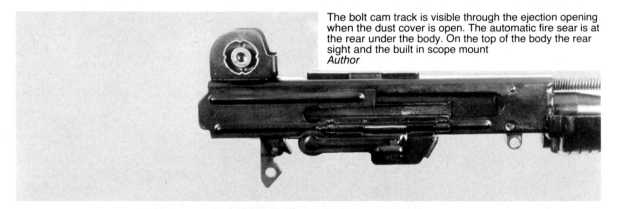

The bolt cam track is visible through the ejection opening when the dust cover is open. The automatic fire sear is at the rear under the body. On the top of the body the rear sight and the built in scope mount
Author

The wedge shaped scope mount and the two position rear aperture sight
Author

The rear sight raised and the cocking handle folded
forward
Author

The Bren Gun

In the early 1930s the British army were looking for
a new light machine gun. The Vickers Berthier was
the favourite when the British Military Attache in
Czechoslovakia reported that he had seen a new
light machine gun, the ZB26 being test fired and
was very impressed. Very surprisingly Whitehall not
only listened to the report but also took action to
obtain weapons for test. The gun was chambered
for the 7·92mm which was a rimless round much
more suited for automatic weapons than the ·303
with its large rim.

Unfortunately when the government decided to
adopt the ZB26 in a modified form they chose for
reasons of economy to change it to use the British
round. The magnitude of this task can be gauged by
the fact that it took from January 1935 until
September 1937 for the guns to be built in prototype
quantity. The weapon was named the Bren after
BRno and ENfield. Throughout its four marks and
indeed conversion to 7·62mm NATO, the weapon
changed little.

The Bren is a gas operated weapon, firing from an
open bolt and fed from a box magazine. The
wartime construction is to a good standard and
indeed the weapon established an enviable
reputation for total reliability in any conditions. The
barrel is easily interchanged by the rotation of the
barrel nut and drawing the barrel forward off the gas
system. The barrel has attached a four-way
adjustable gas plug that can be altered if the
weapon stops from dirt, etc. The weapon is
operated in the following fashion: the weapon is
cocked and the bolt held to the rear by the trigger.
When the trigger is pressed the bolt moves forward
under the pressure of the recoil spring and carries
with it the piston. On picking up a cartridge it
chambers it and the tilting block moves up into the
locking recess in the body. The weapon fires and
the gas forces back the piston that cams the tilting
block downwards out of engagement allowing the
bolt to return rearward and eject the empty case.
The firing pin is designed with a chisel point to the
left to ensure that the primer cannot be blown out
and jam the gun. The sights are offset because of
the top mounted magazine. The rear sight is an
adjustable aperture and the front a blade. The
weapon can fire either single shot or fully auto. The
interchangeable barrel allows almost continuous fire
with no danger of overheating.

The Bren Mk 2
Author

The drum adjusted rear sight, fire selector and barrel release are all on the left of the gun and the magazine release on top
Author

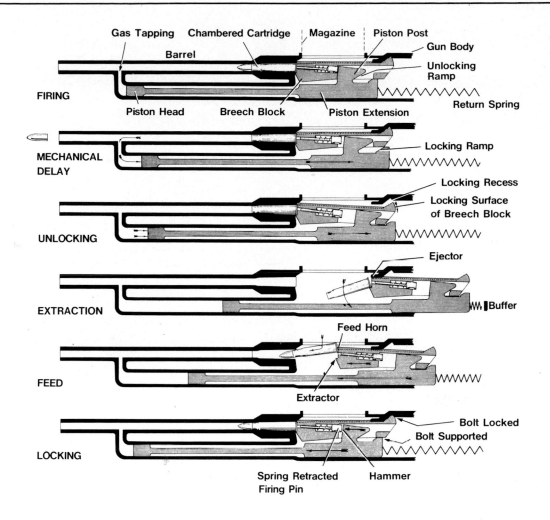

Bren Gun— Action

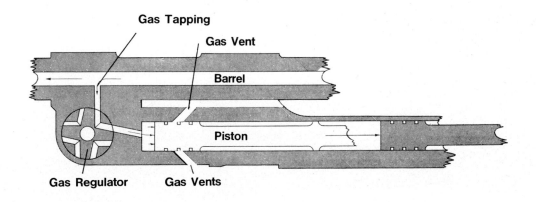

Bren Gun— Gas System

The flash hider and front sight mount on the Mk 1
Author

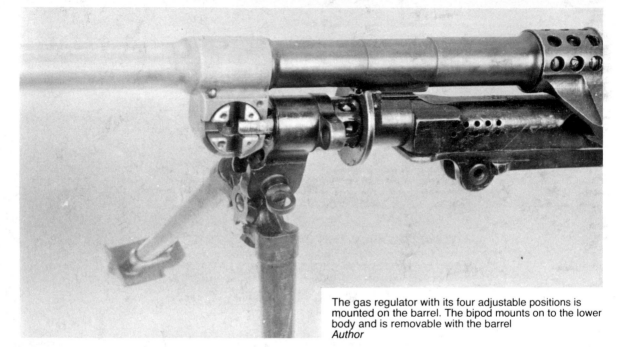

The gas regulator with its four adjustable positions is mounted on the barrel. The bipod mounts on to the lower body and is removable with the barrel
Author

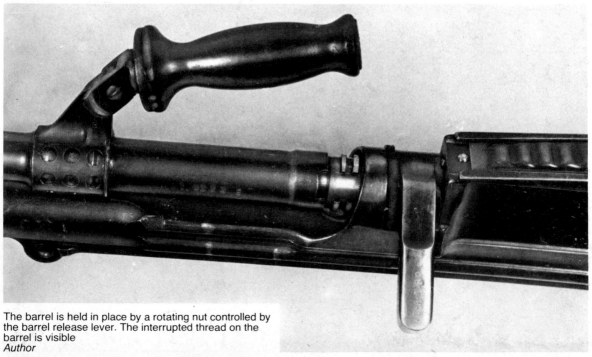

The barrel is held in place by a rotating nut controlled by the barrel release lever. The interrupted thread on the barrel is visible
Author

The Stoner 63 weapon system that was designed by Stoner to enable a basic weapon to be converted to a carbine, rifle, light machine gun, and remote controlled gun. The result has unfortunately been a series of compromises

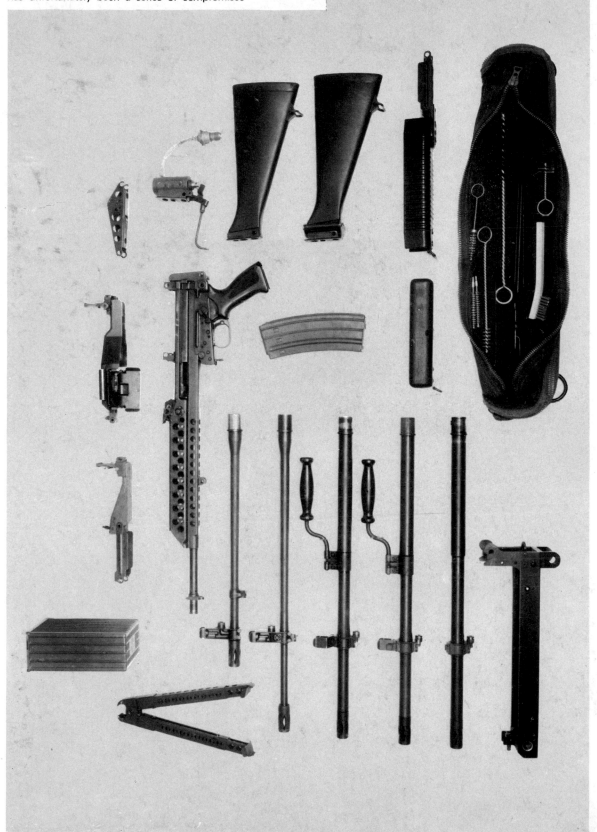

Pistol model 3.000 with gold damascened finish. This pistol was a gift to Argentina's President Juan D. Peron in 1945.
Astra